D0051813

communication
skills for teens

how to
listen,
express &
connect for
success

MICHELLE SKEEN, PsyD | MATTHEW McKAY, PhD
PATRICK FANNING | KELLY SKEEN

"I can't think of a teen, or even an adult, who wouldn't benefit from reading this book. Teens will appreciate the enjoyable flow as well as the relevance of the information and voice. Page by page, easily absorbed concepts increase social intelligence while simply presented tips and strategies increase communication skills. Before I knew it, I was completely through the book and communicating more effectively myself, with more awareness and depth of presence. Yes!"

—**Lucie Hemmen, PhD**, licensed clinical psychologist, author of *Parenting a Teen Girl* and *The Teen Girl's Survival Guide*, and mother of two teen girls

"*Communication Skills for Teens* is brimming with tools for success. Do you know how to express your needs without stepping on toes or cheating yourself? How to handle hidden agendas? How to get past your jitters and break the ice with new people? This book answers these questions and so many more. It is more than a practical book for teens; it's a great communication book for anyone. It will be required reading for my young daughter—as soon as I'm done with it!"

—**Shawn T. Smith, PsyD**, author of *The User's Guide to the Human Mind*

"*Communication Skills for Teens* provides practical skills that you can use right away to listen and speak more clearly, more effectively, and with less chance of unnecessary hurt feelings and misunderstandings. The real-life teen examples will illustrate how you can use these skills in your everyday life to develop stronger and happier relationships with your friends, peers, parents, and adults."

—**Dzung X. Vo, MD**, author of *The Mindful Teen*

"Michelle and Kelly have made *the guide* for interpersonal effectiveness. As a therapist, I will be recommending this book to teens, parents, and adults. Their tone is genuine, the stories are real, and the tools are invaluable. In today's digital world, communicating can be difficult. This book gives you the tools to feel secure in any interaction you face—online or in person."

> —**Emily Roberts, MA, LPC**, psychotherapist and
> author of *Express Yourself*

"This is the missing manual so many of us wish we'd had in our confusing, turbulent teenage years. Even as an adult, I walked away with more effective communication skills for myself as well as my teen clients."

> —**Christopher Willard, PsyD**, author of *Child's Mind*
> and *Mindfulness for Teen Anxiety*, Cambridge Health
> Alliance/Harvard Medical School

"In a world that has evolved into a culture of disengagement, it's refreshing to see such a thoughtful tool that both teaches and encourages teens to authentically connect with one another. The *Communication Skills for Teens* workbook offers excellent, relatable activities to help teens learn the art and skill of sound communication."

> —**Julia V. Taylor, MA**, author of *The Body Image Workbook
> for Teens*, *Salvaging Sisterhood*, and *Perfectly You*, and
> coauthor of *G.I.R.L.S. (Girls in Real Life Situations)* and
> *The Bullying Workbook for Teens*

"A great resource for parents and professionals wanting to understand and help teens to communicate. The addition of a teen as a coauthor provides a unique and down-to-earth reflection on key communication styles. [*Communication Skills for Teens*] goes beyond active listening to provide a comprehensive range of communication patterns and situations. [The book] explains step by step the different ways we communicate our feelings, needs, and beliefs, and then provides exercises to help young people practice the skills."

> —**Louise Hayes, PhD**, clinical psychologist, academic, and coauthor of *The Thriving Adolescent* and *Get Out of Your Mind and Into Your Life for Teens*

"Learning healthy and effective communication skills at an early age is one of the best tools for creating success in life. This book is the perfect guide for teens. The authors' wise advice can be implemented immediately. I highly recommend *Communication Skills for Teens*, not only for adolescents, but for their parents and teachers as well."

> —**Alan C. Fox**, author of the *New York Times* bestseller *People Tools, People Tools for Business,* and *People Tools for Love and Relationships*

"*Communication Skills for Teens* is an invaluable and solid resource for helping teens navigate through life by teaching them the fundamentals of effective communication. Many of today's teens heavily rely on social networking and social media outlets as a means to connect and express themselves. These electronic devices will never replace the value of face-to-face interactions. *Communication Skills for Teens* provides a wealth of information to help teens master the art of in-person communication. This is a book that every teen would benefit from reading!"

> —**Raychelle Cassada Lohmann, MS, LPC**, counselor,
> author of *The Anger Workbook for Teens*, and coauthor
> of *The Bullying Workbook for Teens* and *The Sexual
> Trauma Workbook for Teen Girls*

"*Communication Skills for Teens* is an excellent book for helping teens learn how to cooperate with others and build friendship and love. Practitioners will find the book to be a useful adjunct to therapy, especially when helping teens who have social phobia or other socially based problems."

> —**Joseph Ciarrochi**, professor at the Institute for Positive
> Psychology and Education at Australian Catholic University,
> and coauthor of *The Thriving Adolescent* and the best-selling
> *Get Out of Your Mind and Into Your Life for Teens*

the *i* n s t a n t h e l p
s o l u t i o n s s e r i e s

Young people today need mental health resources more than ever. That's why New Harbinger created the **Instant Help Solutions Series** especially for teens. Written by leading psychologists, physicians, and professionals, these evidence-based self-help books offer practical tips and strategies for dealing with a variety of mental health issues and life challenges teens face, such as depression, anxiety, bullying, eating disorders, trauma, and self-esteem problems.

Studies have shown that young people who learn healthy coping skills early on are better able to navigate problems later in life. Engaging and easy-to-use, these books provide teens with the tools they need to thrive—at home, at school, and on into adulthood.

This series is part of the **New Harbinger Instant Help Books** imprint, founded by renowned child psychologist Lawrence Shapiro. For a complete list of books in this series, visit newharbinger.com.

communication
skills for teens

how to listen, express & connect for success

MICHELLE SKEEN, PsyD
MATTHEW McKAY, PhD
PATRICK FANNING
KELLY SKEEN

Instant Help Books
An Imprint of New Harbinger Publications, Inc.

Distributed in Canada by Raincoast Books

Copyright © 2016 by Michelle Skeen, Matthew McKay, Patrick Fanning,
            and Kelly Skeen
            Instant Help Books
            An Imprint of New Harbinger Publications, Inc.
            5674 Shattuck Avenue
            Oakland, CA 94609
            www.newharbinger.com

Cover design by Amy Shoup
Acquired by Tesilya Hanauer
Edited by Jasmine Star

Library of Congress Cataloging-in-Publication Data

Skeen, Michelle, author.
  Communication skills for teens : how to listen, express, and connect for success / Michelle Skeen, Matthew McKay, Patrick Fanning, and Kelly Skeen.
    pages cm. -- (The instant help solutions series)
  ISBN 978-1-62625-263-9 (pbk. : alk. paper) -- ISBN 978-1-62625-264-6 (pdf e-book) -- ISBN 978-1-62625-265-3 (epub) 1. Interpersonal communication in adolescence--Juvenile literature. 2. Interpersonal communication--Juvenile literature. I. Title.
  BF724.3.I55S54 2016
  155.5'136--dc23

                      2015028415

Printed in the United States of America

18   17   16

10   9   8   7   6   5   4   3   2   1   First Printing

My sons Eric and Jake

—Michelle

My daughter Bekah

—Matt

My son Michael

—Patrick

My Daddio

—Kelly

Contents

Acknowledgments

This book would not have been possible without Matt McKay and Patrick Fanning. These two remarkable men co-founded New Harbinger over forty years ago. They have written dozens of books over the years, but never a teen book. Their book *Messages* was the inspiration for this one, so I wanted them on board for the project. To that end, I decided on a classic wine-and-dine strategy. I had them over for dinner to pitch the book idea. Unfortunately, my culinary skills were seriously impaired, so that aspect of the evening was a fail, but we did have fun decorating gingerbread houses. And, they said yes to coauthoring their first teen book. Thank you, Matt and Pat!

I also want to thank the entire New Harbinger family for supporting this project. There are so many individuals who nurtured this book from the beginning to the end and they were all a joy to work with.

And a very special shout-out to Jasmine Star, our editor extraordinaire. Her edits, queries, and suggestions made *Communication Skills for Teens* a better book. Thank you!

Last but not least, to all teens: you are an inspiring population bursting with fresh ideas, energy, and enthusiasm; it is important that your voices be heard and that your contributions be felt. This book is for you!

—Michelle Skeen

Introduction

Communication is an essential life skill. Effective and healthy communication plays a huge role in success and happiness in life. We communicate in all sorts of ways—body language, facial expression, tone of voice, physical action, and even thoughts—whether we're aware of it or not. Everything we do sends a message about who we are. And others are often making decisions and judgments about us based upon how they perceive us. Therefore, it's vital to bring awareness to the messages that you're communicating about yourself.

Your generation is unique, having grown up with technology and social media unlike anything available to previous generations. This has changed the way people communicate, particularly teens. For many people, face-to-face communication has become secondary to Facebook, Twitter, Instagram, Snapchat, and texting. But as people become more connected to smartphones and the Internet, their ability to connect in person can be compromised, and it may be more difficult to develop effective communication skills. Technology is remarkable, but it doesn't replace the need for effective communication skills. In fact, successful business and personal relationships depend on connecting with people.

This book provides communication skills and guidance that will enable you to thrive in your life and in your relationships. The skills include active listening, self-disclosure, expressing your needs, recognizing your hidden agendas, clarification, assertive communication, making new connections, sexual communication, family communication, and interviewing skills.

Detailed explanations and exercises will help you determine which skills you need to develop or polish in order to increase your ability to communicate clearly and effectively in all aspects of your life. To maximize the benefits, we recommend that you complete the exercises presented in the book. You'll need a journal or notebook for this—or you can use a document on your computer. Choose whatever format you're most comfortable with.

This book is written so that you can work through the chapters in any order you wish. For example, you might decide to start with chapter 8 if you're facing a situation that requires you to communicate about sex. However, we strongly encourage you to read chapter 1 first, since it introduces skills that are referred to in other chapters. Of course, you can also read the chapters in order, from beginning to end. In addition, you may find that you're already more skilled in some areas than others. However, even if you think you're a great listener, we urge you to go ahead and read chapter 1, How to Really Listen, because we've found that it's easy to fall into some of the traps associated with listening.

Before we begin, we'd like to share some information about who wrote this book. Matt McKay and Patrick Fanning wrote a communication skills book for adults, *Messages*, that continues to be a great resource. In fact, Michelle Skeen found it extremely helpful when writing two of her previous books. This inspired her to write a similar book for teens—something she especially cares about because she has a teenage daughter, Kelly (along with two older sons). But Michelle and Kelly agreed that teens don't need more adults in their lives giving them advice and sometimes talking down to them or providing examples that are relevant to adults but don't resonate with younger people. So Kelly became a coauthor, adding a teen's voice and perspective; she provided all of the examples and used her own experiences to gear the book more toward teens. In addition to the material in the book, you can find more content and resources on the book's website: http://www.communicationskillsforteens.com.

So, now that you have a sense of what this book is about and who we are, let's get started!

chapter 1

How to Really Listen

Listening is an essential communication tool. The ability to really hear people is a crucial skill for making and keeping good relationships. Effective listening can also be a game changer during difficult or emotional conversations.

Have you ever had the experience of being in a group where everyone wants to tell their own story and you feel like nobody is truly listening to what others are saying? Even when people appear to be listening closely, you can see that they're actually just rehearsing what they want to say and waiting for their chance to talk. Other times people are distracted, perhaps with their eyes wandering to their phone or computer.

To build relationships, it's important to really listen to others. If you're a good listener, others will be drawn to you. Your friends will confide in you, and you'll make new friends more easily. In school or job situations, you may experience success more quickly or easily if you really hear people and understand them. You can grasp what others expect from you, what's important to them, and what pleases or displeases them. Not listening well suggests that you don't care, that you aren't interested in what others have to say, or that you're self-absorbed.

Listening is a skill like anything else, so the more you practice, the better you'll become. Really hearing others requires a commitment to empathy and a willingness to understand someone else's feelings and point of view. Good listening is easier if you can be open and hear without judgment.

In short, listening well builds strong relationships because it shows that you care.

Real Listening vs. Pseudo Listening

We've all been guilty of pseudo listening, or half listening. With so many distractions in our environment, it's easy to fall into pseudo listening. The first step in combating this common habit is to understand the distinction between real listening and pseudo listening.

Real listening is more than just being quiet while the other person is talking. It involves four distinct intentions:

* **To understand** what the other person is saying, without imposing your own judgments

* **To enjoy** your interaction and appreciate that the person is sharing a part of himself or herself with you

* **To learn** more about the other person, including the person's thoughts, feelings, and opinions

* **To help**, which involves paying particular attention to ways in which you can assist the person or provide support

Listening to others with these intentions in mind will result in more successful interactions. Having a desire to understand makes you pay attention. The expectation of enjoyment helps you engage and focus. The hope of learning something new stimulates your mind. And wanting to help creates a caring and empathic exchange.

* **kelly** * There are many times when my own thoughts get in the way of truly listening to others. At any given time when I'm hanging out with friends or family, I may also be somewhere else—for example, using my phone to send and read texts or check social media. At those times, even though I may hear every word others are saying, I'm not absorbing what I'm hearing. Because I don't process what they're saying, I can't respond in a meaningful way. Sometimes the solution is as simple as leaving my phone in my bag.

However, there are some distractions I can't control as easily, like being caught up in my own problems. That can interfere with truly hearing someone. For example, the other day a friend was asking for my advice on a difficult situation she was experiencing with her parents. While I cared about her problem, I was feeling overwhelmed by two big projects I had to turn in the next day. I knew I wouldn't be able to give her good feedback in the moment, so I asked her if we could meet up the next day. That way, my deadlines wouldn't interfere with my ability to be a good listener and a caring friend.

Exercise: Looking for Patterns in Your Listening

You can probably think of times when your issues or concerns have inter-fered with fully hearing someone else. Look for patterns in your listening and record them in your journal. Notice when you do well and are listening with at least one of the four intentions: to understand, to enjoy, to learn, or to help. Also notice how often you slip into pseudo listening. Then identify environments, situations, or people that tend to make real listening easier or more challenging for you.

If you find that it's difficult for you to genuinely focus in certain set-tings, move important conversations from those settings to places where you can listen more effectively. Likewise, if real listening isn't possible in the moment, suggest another time for the conversation that works well for everyone involved.

Blocks to Listening

Blocks to listening prevent you from hearing people. Everybody is prone to listening blocks, so don't feel bad about having them; it's human nature. But once you become aware of your listen-ing patterns, you can more easily avoid the blocks and become a better listener.

In this section you'll learn about the twelve most common blocks to listening. You probably fall into some of them fre-quently, and those are likely to sound very familiar.

Comparing. When you're busy comparing yourself to people who are talking to you, you're not hearing them. Instead, you're trying to figure out if you're as smart, as good-looking, as funny, as tough, and so on. Regardless of whether you're making positive or negative comparisons, you're not focused on hearing the other person. It's easy to get caught up in how you measure up to others in particular settings or situations. Again, that's human nature; we can't help but compare ourselves to others. However, we can bring awareness to noticing when it occurs and then not let it get in the way of listening well.

Mind reading. This is a very common listening block. When you're mind reading, you're paying less attention to the actual words people are saying and too much attention to their tone of voice and body language in an effort to figure out their thoughts and feelings. For example, you may find yourself imagining what the other person is thinking about you instead of listening to what the person is saying.

Rehearsing. It's tempting to start thinking about crafting your response to others while they're still talking. But when you do that, you're likely to miss out on important information that they're trying to communicate to you.

* kelly * I fall into the trap of rehearsing in icebreaker situations. When I arrived for my first semester of college, I must have played at least twenty different icebreaker games. For example, in one, everyone in the group had to fill in the statement "If you really knew me, you'd know..." with an intriguing piece of information

about themselves. Of course, everyone, including me, felt
pressured to come up with something our peers would
find interesting and entertaining. So instead of paying
attention to other people's contributions, I was busy
figuring out what I would share.

Filtering. You know you're filtering if you consistently pay attention to some things more than others. For example, you may be less interested in the content of what others are communicating than figuring out whether they're in a good mood or a bad mood. Some people filter for material that's critical of them, some for compliments, some for a particular topic that interests them, and so on. Filtering can also involve excluding some types of information, leading people to listen selectively, ignoring remarks that are of little or no interest to them.

Judging. If you're too quick to pass judgment on people, you won't hear what they're actually saying. Be careful not to judge people on their appearance or what you've heard about them. Stay open to the content they're communicating, rather than dismissing them because you have preconceived notions about them.

Daydreaming. This is a particularly problematic listening block because when you're daydreaming, you're completely focused on other things, not the person in front of you. You won't be able to make a valuable connection if you're tuned out.

Identifying. This listening block can grow out of a desire to connect about a shared experience. But when you're too busy focusing on how your experience relates to what others are saying, it starts to become more about you and less about them.

> ✳ **kelly** ✳ Identifying is a listening block that's one of my greatest challenges in communicating with others. My intention is to create a stronger bond with people I'm talking to, but I've realized that it makes them feel as though they aren't being fully heard. It can also make me seem self-absorbed.

Advising. Like identifying, advising is often based on a desire to connect. Unfortunately, it can make others feel like you're too focused on trying to offer a solution and as though you aren't allowing them to finish communicating their entire experience or situation.

Arguing. When you're focused on promoting or defending your opinions and beliefs, it's difficult to make genuine connections with others. Arguing alienates people because it sends a message that you're not open to understanding their point of view and what they have to say.

Being right. This listening block is a huge obstacle to connecting with other people. It's hard to learn from others or grow in terms of your beliefs and feelings if you aren't open to other people's opinions.

Derailing. This listening block involves quickly changing the topic to avoid criticism or talking about something that makes you anxious or upset. Sometimes people derail conversations by making jokes or distracting comments. Of course, this gets in the way of making a meaningful connection with others.

Placating. You may do this in an effort to be liked, agreeing with everything the other person says or does. However, it's difficult to connect with others if you're focused on making sure they feel good. If you're placating, you aren't tuned in to or examining what the other person is saying.

Exercise: Identifying Your Listening Blocks

We all get trapped by listening blocks, whether we do so knowingly or unknowingly. The first step to improving relationships is to bring awareness to the things that are getting in the way of clear communication. Take some time to think about and identify your primary listening blocks and the situations or people associated with them, then record this information in your journal. Also think about situations or places in which your listening blocks tend to come up most often. For example, you might find that at home with your parents you're more likely to argue, at school with teachers you're more into placating, and that while hanging out with friends you have a tendency to focus on trying to be right.

With practice, you can largely overcome these blocks and become a better listener. This will result in more interesting, satisfying, and meaningful interactions with the people in your life.

✳ kelly ✳ I find that I'm a better listener when I stay in the moment and have an open mind. I try to wait until others have finished speaking before I come to a conclusion about what they're saying. That way I can understand their perspective more fully. Also, when I'm having an important conversation with someone, I make sure I'm completely focused on that person, not on other things, like friends passing by.

Active Listening

Now that you're familiar with the most common listening blocks, let's take a look at how you can become a more effective listener in all of your interactions, whether with friends, siblings, parents, teachers, or others. The key is to engage in active listening, which is a three-step process:

1. Paraphrasing

2. Clarifying

3. Providing feedback

Active listening is a necessary skill for building relationships. It requires that you be fully engaged in the process of communicating and aware of the listening blocks you just identified. It also means responding with your words, body language, and eye contact—all ways of indicating that you're engaged in the conversation.

Step 1. Paraphrasing

Paraphrasing is using your own words to restate what someone else has said. This prevents miscommunication, false assumptions, and misunderstandings. It also makes conversations easier to remember. Here are a few ways to lead into a paraphrase:

* "So in other words..."

* "I get that you..."

* "What I hear you saying is..."

* "What happened was that..."

* "So you're saying..."

Paraphrasing focuses your attention on the actual content of what others are saying. In this way, it helps prevent most of the listening blocks described in the previous section, like rehearsing your next remark or preparing an argument against something that's been said.

There are many advantages to paraphrasing. One is that it conveys that you're really listening. You may be surprised at how much others appreciate being heard. Also, if others are upset or angry, paraphrasing is a good way to calm them down. And if what someone is saying is unclear, paraphrasing will prevent miscommunication and misinterpretation. Finally, as mentioned, paraphrasing helps you remember what was said.

* **kelly** * If I'm involved in any kind of conflict, I find that paraphrasing helps me solve the problem more smoothly. Whenever I have a disagreement with one of my friends, I can ease the tension by paraphrasing his or her concerns. This really makes people feel heard.

Step 2. Clarifying

Clarifying is an extension of paraphrasing. It involves asking questions until you have a clear understanding of what's being said. This allows you to get more information to fill in any gaps in the communication. Ultimately, clarifying sends the message that you're engaged in communicating and that you care about the person and the situation.

* **kelly** * One time my mom was going out for the evening and said my brothers and I could invite "a few people over." When she got home, she was stunned that there were a few *dozen* people there. If we had clarified what she meant by "a few," we would have avoided a very unpleasant family meeting.

Step 3. Feedback

The final piece of active listening is feedback. After you've paraphrased what you heard and asked clarifying questions, it's your turn to add something new: your personal reaction. With feedback, you express what you think and feel about what you heard and your experience while listening.

This is when you get a chance to present your point of view, but without arguing, advising, derailing, and so on. There are three main qualities that good feedback should have: it should be immediate, honest, and supportive. "Immediate" means providing your reaction right away; don't wait until an hour or a day later, and then text your reaction. The most valuable feedback is what you say right after paraphrasing and clarifying, when the topic is fresh and you and the other person are on the same page.

As for honesty and supportiveness, feedback should be truthful without being hurtful. Even negative feedback can be delivered in a gentle, supportive way. For example, instead of saying, "You're hiding something," you could say, "I get the feeling there's something you're not telling me. I'm here for you."

Listening with Empathy, Openness, and Awareness

Your communication with others will also be enhanced if you bring certain qualities to listening: empathy, openness, and awareness.

Listening with Empathy

The key to listening with empathy is to imagine being in the other person's shoes and feeling what he or she is feeling. This doesn't mean you have to agree with the way another person handled a situation. In fact, you need to steer clear of focusing on how you would have felt or acted if you'd been in the same situation. Instead, take the perspective of the other person and try to understand what that person may be feeling and thinking.

Listening with empathy will enhance your relationships and allow you to create deeper connections with others. Taking this kind of perspective will also help you learn more about yourself and others.

Listening with Openness

Listening with openness means listening without judging or finding fault with what you hear. If you have a closed mind, you won't be able to hear the other person's whole message because you'll be focused on how it's inconsistent with your own thoughts, feelings, and beliefs.

Everybody has trouble listening openly. One way to foster this approach is to think of yourself as a scientist. Say to yourself, "I value the truth. I want to know what's what, even if it means changing my opinion. My opinions are simply my current theories about life, and they're subject to revision as new information becomes available." Be curious. It will help you remain open.

Listening with Awareness

Listening with awareness is where using your ability to judge and compare things is appropriate. The first half of listening with awareness is to compare what you hear with your knowledge about the past, people, and the way things work. You're not evaluating what others are saying; you're just comparing what they say to known facts. This has the added benefit of keeping you focused on the details of what others are saying.

The second half of listening with awareness is to look for consistency and congruence between what people say and how they act. Notice their body language, in the form of posture, gestures, and facial expressions. Pay attention to their tone of voice and how loudly or softly they're speaking. Sometimes there's an obvious mismatch. For example, maybe someone is telling you that his dog got hit by a car, but he's on the couch with his hands behind his head, yawning and talking in a soft, relaxed tone. When something like this happens, you can ask for clarification or give feedback: "It seems to me that you're not very upset. Wasn't it sad?"

Putting It All Together

One of the keys to creating and maintaining healthy and successful relationships is to actively engage with others. This requires that you be a good listener. Specifically, it means not engaging in pseudo listening or getting trapped by listening blocks too often. It also means not letting your own thoughts, feelings, beliefs, and judgments distort what others are saying. Using active listening and communicating through body language, eye contact, and thoughtful responses or questions demonstrates that you're paying attention and that you care. It's also vital to bring certain qualities to listening and communicating.

Empathizing with others can help you create more meaningful relationships. Being open to thoughts and beliefs that differ from your own will promote your ongoing evolution as a person. And listening with awareness will allow you to understand and connect more easily.

chapter 2

Letting Others Know You

Your relationships with friends, family members, people you date, and others you care about are hugely important. These are the people you share good times with, who support and care about you, and who help you feel connected and not alone. The strength of your relationships has a lot to do with how happy you feel. And how much you let people in so they can know you has a lot to do with the strength of your relationships. So in this chapter, we'll focus on using self-disclosure, or sharing information about yourself, to build your relationships.

The Rewards of Self-Disclosure

Self-disclosure can have a lot of benefits. This isn't just our opinion; it's something that has been shown by research into communication. Here are some of the rewards you may experience, based on research summarized in the book *Messages*, by Matthew McKay, Martha Davis, and Patrick Fanning:

* Sharing some of your needs, feelings, and experiences creates more closeness and mutual commitment. You don't have to disclose everything that

happens to you, just enough for the other person to feel trusted and let in.

* The more people know you, the more they tend to like you. This is the opposite of what we often fear: "When they know me, they'll see my flaws."

* When you let people in and they get to know you, those relationships feel safer. You're less afraid that others will discover something about you that turns them off. As a result, you can relax and enjoy each other more.

* Relationships in which you're known and understood tend to be more supportive. Friends and even family members will do more for the people they know well, so they're more likely to show up when you need them.

* Friendships often last longer when they're built on real sharing. People in these kinds of relationships care about each other more, and conflicts and other obstacles aren't as likely to damage the relationship.

* People are likely to treat you better if you've shared what supports you and what hurts you. When others know how you feel, they tend to be more careful not to do things that bring you down.

* The more you let people in and the better they know you, the less alone you're likely to feel.

The Path to Self-Disclosure

So here's the question: If sharing and letting people in can promote stronger relationships, how do you do it? And maybe more importantly, how do you let people in without ending up feeling humiliated or risking rejection? The answer is to proceed gradually.

Let's start by looking at the types of things people share and disclose in relationships. Here are some of them, listed from least to most risky.

Preferences and interests. These are things you like or dislike, such as a favorite band or a teacher you can't stand. This can extend to styles, places, activities, celebrities, subjects for conversation, or even, at a more risky level, things you like more or less about yourself. Sharing your preferences and interests often creates an instant feeling of closeness, and it usually encourages others to do the same.

Information. This is basic stuff like which classes you're taking, whether you play sports, what you do after school, what bus you take, or the neighborhood where you live. This kind of sharing is also pretty low risk. It doesn't usually give people much of a basis on which to judge you, but it does give them the feeling that they're getting to know you.

Your history. At the low-risk end, this would include funny or interesting stories from your past—things that happened to you that could keep a conversation going or would just be fun to share. At a deeper level, you might share hard or painful things you've experienced in life, perhaps challenges or crises you had to face. Although sharing your struggles may feel more dangerous, it's a great way to build trust. People tend to feel safer and closer to others who share about some of the not-so-great things they've gone through.

Opinions. How you think about and evaluate things is important. Some of your opinions come from deep within you and reflect how you truly see the world. Close, trusting relationships are partly built on each person knowing how the other sees things. Imagine trying to connect to someone who says nothing about what he or she thinks or believes. It would probably be uncomfortable because you'd have no clue as to where the person is coming from. Being willing to share some of your opinions—even on lightweight subjects—will help your relationships feel safer and deeper.

Values. Similar to opinions, but more personal and important, are your values. Your values reflect what you really care about and how you want to live your life. (We will explore values in greater depth in chapter 8.) They can include how you want to act and be with people you care about, what you want to do with your life, and things you feel really committed to. Values might also involve what you want for the world and what you think people should do for others. Because values feel so important, they may not be a good choice for the lead topic with a new friend. But sharing some of your values may help you take a big step toward developing a closer relationship.

* **kelly** * Whenever I've started at a new school, in both high school and college, making worthwhile friendships has been a priority for me. But recently, after a few months of hanging out with a group of friends, I realized I wasn't really in the mood to go out with them as much anymore. When I thought about it, I realized that my values differ from theirs. For most of them, going out and partying on the weekends is really important. I enjoy socializing, but I also want to get up early on Sunday morning to go for a run or hike. That doesn't mean I can't be friends with them, but it was helpful for me to recognize the limits of those relationships.

What you want. This is a big topic that can take you in many different directions. There are things you wanted in the past, and things you want for your future. Some might be simple, like a new sketch pad or a video game. Others might be a deep yearning, like wanting to spend more time with your dad after your parents' divorce. Future desires might have to do with a career you dream of, or just the hope you won't have to take chemistry next year. Sharing some of the things you want adds depth to a relationship. It can also encourage reciprocal sharing by others. That's a huge payoff. When others share their desires, you feel let in. You feel a deeper connection.

Feelings from the past. These are the fabric of your life—moments of hope, sadness, fear, love, or anger that you've experienced. This includes past feelings about yourself or your relationships. Sharing positive emotions is less risky, so it usually feels safer to start there. But sharing vulnerable or painful emotions can feel like a relief because someone finally knows and understands what you went through. When sharing about darker emotions, start with a brief mention. See if the other person shows interest and a willingness to listen. After testing the water, you may choose to go deeper.

Here-and-now experience. Finally, at the riskier end of the spectrum, you can share about what you feel or want in the moment. You can take a less risky approach by sharing about your feelings or needs related to someone other than the person you're talking to. Perhaps the most difficult things to share are feelings or needs regarding the person you're interacting with. This is scary because it risks rejection. But putting your feelings and needs out in the open can also change relationships in amazing ways. For example, saying something like "This has been fun; I'd like to spend more time hanging out" can lead to painful feelings if it turns out that the other person thinks the relationship isn't going anywhere. But it could result in a closer, deeper connection if the other person wants that too. Given that sharing even positive feelings can be so challenging, negative here-and-now emotions are probably the most difficult thing to talk about. If you don't, however, and the feelings persist, they can create a silent rift that a relationship may never recover from.

Sharing isn't easy for many of us. Maybe you've been shamed, criticized, or teased in the past, just for being you. If so, you've probably learned to hide yourself. In this case, the risk of sharing may feel enormous. Yet the cost of not sharing can be just as big. True friendship depends on sharing some of who you are, what you think, and what you care about.

Assessing Your Openness

How much do you let people in? One way to explore how open you are is an assessment tool called a Johari window.

Imagine that your entire self is represented by a circle divided into four quadrants (to see an illustration, visit http://www.communicationskillsforteens.com). The first quadrant, at the upper left, is the open self. All of the feelings, needs, and experiences in this part of you are transparent—known to you and people you're close to. The second quadrant, at the lower left, is the hidden self. It holds feelings, needs, and experiences that you're aware of but keep from others. The third quadrant, at the upper right, is the blind self, and it includes reactions and feelings that other people can see (perhaps in your body language, tone, or demeanor) but you aren't completely aware of. The fourth and final quadrant, at the lower right, is the unknown self, and it's a big blank. These are experiences you hide from yourself and everyone else.

Everything that happens to you—all your thoughts, feelings, desires, and everything you experience—starts out in the hidden self. Some of this stays in the hidden self. Some of it is forgotten or suppressed and moves into the unknown self.

Some of it takes the form of unconscious but observable reactions rooted in your blind self. And, of course, you share many of your thoughts, feelings, desires, and experiences with others, bringing them into the open self.

The open self is what builds close, strong relationships. The larger this quadrant is with any given person, the stronger and more resilient that relationship is likely to be. You are known and have let the other person in, opening the door to the rewards of self-disclosure outlined earlier in this chapter.

One thing that's interesting about the Johari window is that content can be moved from quadrant to quadrant. At any given time and in any given relationship, more of you may be open or hidden.

Many people have a goal of hiding as little as possible from themselves, keeping their blind and unknown quadrants relatively small. However, people are very different in terms of how much they keep hidden or reveal to others. A larger hidden self usually corresponds to larger unknown self, and vice versa. Sometimes having a larger open self indicates that a person just puts more of himself or herself out there, perhaps without being aware of what he or she is revealing. In this case, a larger open self corresponds to a larger blind self.

Exercise: Exploring Your Openness with Johari Windows

Right now, on half a page in your journal, create a Johari window depicting the relative sizes of your open, hidden, blind, and unknown selves. For now, just draw a general representation, not specific to particular relationships. Then, on the other half of the page, draw another Johari window, this time showing the size of each of the four quadrants if you could be exactly how you want to be.

As mentioned in the preceding section, how open or hidden you are can vary from relationship to relationship. That's often appropriate: some people deserve more of you than others, and it can be risky to be open with certain people. To explore this, draw two Johari windows for each relationship you'd like to examine. For each, adjust the size of the panes in the first drawing to indicate how much you let the other person in now. Adjust the size of the panes in the second drawing to indicate how open you'd like to be in this relationship. It's quite possible that your current level of self-disclosure is exactly where you want it to be in some relationships. In other relationships, you might prefer to be more open or hidden depending on what you hope to achieve. With some people, it may feel safer to be more hidden. But with friends or family, where you want a deeper, more honest connection, you might prefer to expand the upper left quadrant— your open self.

Exercise: Exploring Your Levels of Openness

Another way to explore the degree to which you let people in is to examine the things you share and the people you share them with. You can create a table in your journal to do this (or visit the book website, http://www.communi cationskillsforteens.com, where you'll find a table you can print out for this exercise). To create the table, along the left-hand side, write the areas of self-disclosure we listed earlier: your preferences and interests, basic information, your history, your opinions, your values, what you want (in either the future or the past), feelings from the past, and your here-and-now experience. Then, across the top, list key people in your life, such as your parents, siblings, best friend, boyfriend or girlfriend, friends, acquaintances, and teachers or mentors.

For each part of yourself you share (preferences, information, history, and so on), write 0, 1, or 2 under each relationship you've listed (mother, brother, best friend, mentor, and so on), using 0 to indicate that you've told the person nothing about this aspect of yourself, 1 to indicate that the two of you talk about this aspect of yourself sometimes or in general terms, and 2 to indicate that you share this part of yourself frequently or completely with the other person. Go ahead and fill in your level of openness with each person in the table.

Now review what you've filled in. For any of the people listed, would you like to change the level of sharing and disclosure? If so, write the number that indicates how much openness you want in the relationship next to the first number you wrote, perhaps using a different color of pen or pencil for the second number.

In this exercise (and the previous one), you've been thinking about your relationships: how open you are in them now and how much disclosure you'd like to have. What do you notice? Are many of your relationships about right in terms of how much you let people in? For some relationships, would you like to have more openness and authenticity than you have now? Are there any relationships where you generally want to share less or feel your current level of disclosure is too dangerous? If so, list any people you'd prefer to share less with in your journal.

Ultimately, the question is which relationships you'd like to enhance and make stronger with more openness. Who would you like to take this chance with? Who's worth the effort and the risk? Circle those relationships in your chart.

✱ **kelly** ✱ Recently, I made a new friend in Spanish class. We haven't spent a lot of time together outside of class, except for working on homework every so often and saying hi to each other at the gym. For this new acquaintance, I wrote down a 2 under preferences and interests and also under information, because we often talk about our classes, wanting to work in a bilingual environment, and our weekend plans. I wrote a 1 under my history because I've told her a few funny stories about my family and home life, but we haven't talked about anything that feels more risky. For items like values, feelings from the past, and my here-and-now experience, I recorded a 0. Doing this exercise in my journal made me think about how I'd like to build my relationship with my new friend and a few ways that I can go about doing that.

Making a Plan for Letting People In

If there are people you'd like to build a closer relationship with, you may find it helpful to have a plan. Here are some guidelines for strengthening your relationships with people who are important to you:

1. Set aside a time when the two of you can talk one-on-one. Groups are fun, but they don't allow for the kind of communication that builds closeness.

2.   Start a typical conversation. If you overshare, saying too much too soon (like "I've been really sad about you lately"), it may put too much pressure on the relationship.

3.   Add something from an area of self-disclosure that you don't usually risk with the person. This could be sharing about a preference, an opinion, or something you feel or want. Plan ahead for this, thinking about how you might transition from a more typical conversation into this deeper area.

4.   Disclose a little bit. Don't take off your clothes psychologically, so to speak. Then see what happens. Is the other person interested? Does the person ask questions? Does the person seem to have any sort of judgment about what you shared? Does the person follow up with his or her own disclosure?

5.   Go slowly; open the door gradually. If the person seems interested and accepting, share more of your experience, once again watching to see what happens. You may want to do this slowly, over the course of several conversations. Each time you go deeper, notice how the relationship feels. Closer? Safer? More caring and supportive? More dangerous? Decide how far to go based on whether the relationship feels better or not.

When using this approach, realize that not all relationships grow stronger when you let people in. Some people don't respond well to closeness. They may get weird or judgmental. That's okay—just accept it and let the relationship exist at whatever level works with that particular person. It's important to invest your relationship energy in the people who are worthy of it—friends and family who reciprocate, accept you, and care about you.

To see how this approach works in real life, consider this example: Allie has a boyfriend—sort of. She likes Garrett, but she's still getting to know him. They met in the triathlon club at their high school, where they bonded over dreading the swim workouts and setting the pace in cycling sessions. They started their friendship by giving each other pointers in training sessions and making jokes to lighten the often intense mood of the club's workouts. For the past month, they've been spending time together on weekends, going out for meals or hiking on Allie's favorite trails with her dog. Recently, Garrett took Allie to a concert in the park when one of her favorite local bands was playing.

After that concert, Allie decided that the next time Garrett came over to her house she'd bring up something more personal with him. She'd been talking to her school counselor about looking into running cross-country in college. She decided to bring it up (sharing about what she wants), introducing the topic by asking Garrett if he'd thought about playing sports in college. She planned in advance that if the conversation went well and Garrett showed an interest in her future plans, she'd tell him about her dad's hesitancy about her pursuing athletics in college (sharing her here-and-now experience). Allie hoped she'd end up feeling closer to Garrett.

She was excited when Garrett mentioned that he'd started to look into triathlon clubs at colleges he was interested in. His response helped her feel comfortable telling him about the issues she'd been experiencing with her dad regarding sports. Her father didn't want her to be a student-athlete because he thought her commitment to the team would be a distraction from her schoolwork. Garrett responded empathetically and helped Allie come up with strategies for showing her dad how much sports mattered to her, and that she could handle all of the demands on her time.

Putting It All Together

In chapter 1, we focused on the importance of listening, including listening with empathy, openness, and awareness. The themes and topic of this chapter underscore how essential it is to listen with empathy. In order to build healthy relationships, you must not only understand the other person's experiences, but connect with them, too. Try to feel what others are feeling and then show them that you understand and care about both their triumphs and their struggles. When you listen with empathy, you open channels of communication and create stronger bonds.

Identifying people in your life you'd like to share parts of yourself with and determining how much of yourself you want to share is a big part of creating and strengthening relationships. It has the added benefit of increasing your self-awareness, since you're likely to understand yourself better when you're more open with others.

chapter 3

Expressing What You Feel and Need

This chapter will teach you how to communicate important information to the people who matter in your life. The approach we'll outline involves using clear, complete statements. By "complete," we mean whole messages that include four key types of information: observations, thoughts, feelings, and needs. After all, no matter how clear your communication, if it's incomplete, others are less likely to understand what you're saying or why it matters to you. There's an art to this approach, so we'll provide specific guidelines for going about it, and a lot of exercises to help you practice it.

Four Kinds of Expression

The information you convey to others generally falls into four distinct categories: observations, thoughts, feelings, and needs. Each kind of expression has its own style and vocabulary.

Observations

Observations are simple facts: who, what, where, when. They seldom involve how and why. When you make an observation, you stick to what you can experience with your five senses. This is the language of the scientist, the detective, or the technician, describing obvious details without speculating or theorizing. Here are some examples of straightforward observations:

* "It's starting to rain."

* "I have jazz band practice until five o'clock on Tuesday and Thursday evenings."

* "In my history textbook, I read a passage that said Adolf Hitler was a vegetarian."

* "I dropped my phone in the bathroom sink yesterday and it isn't turning on."

Each of these statements refers to what the speaker has read, observed, heard, or otherwise personally experienced. There is no interpretation or opinion involved.

Thoughts

Thoughts are the conclusions we draw after observing the facts. They're all about the how and why. Thoughts can be expressed as evaluations or judgments, beliefs, theories, interpretations, or opinions:

* **Evaluation or judgment:** "What Todd said about you was unfair and really rude."

* **Belief:** "Telling the truth is the most important part of a relationship."

* **Theory:** "Maybe he wanted other people to believe something bad about you so they wouldn't focus on his mistakes."

* **Interpretation:** "He only got so upset because he cares about what you think of him."

* **Opinion:** "People who don't feel good about themselves do that a lot."

Notice that thoughts are subjective. They lack the objectivity of an observation, but they express who we are and what we believe based upon our experiences.

Feelings

Feelings are the most difficult kind of information to communicate to others because they can be complex, threatening, scary, and difficult to articulate—even to yourself. Plus, some people are uncomfortable talking or hearing about any kind of emotions. Others can tolerate certain kinds of emotions, like happy or sad feelings, but are terrified by others, like anger. You might find it easier to share your positive emotions than those that are difficult.

Because feelings are so powerful, it's especially important to express them. How you feel is a big part of who you are and what makes you unique. For people to know the real you, they need to understand your emotions. When you let others in on your joys, sorrows, fears, or anger, they're more likely to empathize with you and understand you. They'll also have the information they need to change their behavior to meet your needs—if that's something they want to do. Here are some examples of clear expression of feelings:

* "I feel like I let you down, and it makes me sad."

* "When you didn't show up for the game, I felt disappointed."

* "Lisa moved to Washington, and I feel lonely without her here."

* "When I see you after being apart for a while, I feel so incredibly happy."

Notice that these expressions are about emotions; they aren't judgments, evaluations, or opinions disguised as feelings. Keeping the two types of statements separate and distinct is crucial for effective conversations about how you're feeling. For example, "I feel that you're very careless" isn't really a feeling; it's a judgment disguised as a feeling.

Needs

You're the expert on what you need. Nobody else knows what you need better than you do. Unfortunately, we're often taught that it isn't nice to ask for things, and that we should be unselfish and not put our needs before those of others. In addition, many people seem to have the attitude "If you really loved me, you'd know what I need." Then they get offended when others don't guess what they need. When they finally get fed up and ask for something, they tend to do so with anger and resentment: "I can't believe you didn't recognize that I needed you to meet me after I finished my interview. I wanted you to support me, but now it's obvious that you don't even care."

If you have trouble expressing your needs in a relationship, it's like trying to drive a car without a steering wheel. You can step on the gas or stomp on the brake, but you can't change direction or steer around potholes. In contrast, if you can express your needs clearly and appropriately, your relationships will grow, change, and deepen, becoming more satisfying and supportive. Here are some examples of clear statements of needs:

* "Can you please get here by 6:30 so we can go to that movie I talked about seeing?"

* "I have so much homework to finish. I'd rather hang out on Sunday when I'm not feeling stressed."

* "I really need to talk to you privately. Can we meet up after school?"

Remember, statements of needs don't blame or assign fault to anyone. They're designed to communicate what would help you or please you.

Whole vs. Partial Messages

A whole message includes each of the four kinds of expression: observations, thoughts, feelings, and needs. Whole messages allow others to have a well-rounded picture of you, under-standing you in a more complete and accurate way. Your closest friends, your boyfriend or girlfriend, your family members, and other important people in your life all deserve to hear whole messages from you. This means not leaving things out, even stuff that's hard to talk about, like negative judgments, angry or fearful feelings, and what you truly want and need from others.

A partial message is one that leaves something out and, as a result, causes frustration, confusion, anger, or mistrust. For example, describing only the facts and not providing any interpretation or stating your feelings is often boring for listen-ers. Expressing strong opinions, beliefs, or judgments without any factual observations to back them up can cause frustration or anger. Expressing emotions like anger or fear without any explanation of your thoughts or needs tends to be confusing. And stating your needs by asking someone for support or help without providing any facts or sharing your emotions can lead to resistance or even anger.

Of course, not every interaction requires a whole message. A librarian doesn't need a summary of your hopes and dreams to help you find a book for your research project. A distant rela-tive who asks, "How old are you now, and what grade are you in?" doesn't need to know much more than the bare facts. On the other hand, it's good practice to sometimes provide whole messages even in these kinds of casual interactions. When you say more, it enriches the experience, sometimes resulting in an engaging conversation rather than the boring small talk you might have anticipated.

Exercise: Identifying Whole and Partial Messages

You can test whether your messages are whole or partial by asking yourself these questions:

- **Observations:** Have I expressed the facts as I know them, such as things I've read, seen, or heard?

- **Thoughts:** Have I given my conclusions and opinions and clearly labeled them as my thoughts?

- **Feelings:** Have I shared my emotions clearly, without blaming or judgment?

- **Needs:** Have I expressed my needs clearly, without blaming or judgment?

Take a moment now to recall a recent conversation. Then, in your journal, answer the four questions above. Based on your answers, does your message in that conversation seem whole or partial?

Contaminated Messages

Contaminated messages happen when observations, thoughts, feelings, and needs get jumbled up together or one kind of expression is disguised as another. Contaminated messages are almost always confusing and often very alienating. Here are some examples of contaminated messages in which one kind of expression is disguised as another: feelings masquerading as observations, needs expressed as opinions, and so on.

"You're always so cold and distant." This is a negative feeling, a need, and a judgment disguised as an observation. Unpacking this message into a whole expression would yield something like this: "You barely say anything, and when you do, it's in a flat tone [observation]. It makes me think that you don't care and aren't interested in me [thought]. I feel lonely and hurt [feeling]. I want you to talk to me more [need]."

"Here's an idea: maybe you can do your own homework." This message has the feelings of anger and irritation behind a statement expressed as a thought. A more complete version would be "Two or three times a week you ask to copy my math homework [observation]. You're capable of doing it yourself, but I guess it's easier for you to copy mine [thought]. I feel like you're using me [feeling]. I want you to stop asking to copy my homework and take responsibility for doing it yourself [need]."

"You can't make it? What a surprise!" If you say something like this when a friend changes plans for the thousandth time, it's a statement of need and negative feelings wrapped up in sarcasm. A whole message might sound like this: "Last week you bailed on the movies, the week before you didn't show for the yearbook committee, and now you have a conflict and can't come over to play video games like we planned [observation]. You have a hard time saying no to people, so you overcommit to things and then bail out on me because you know I'll let you get away with it [thought]. That really disappoints me and makes me mad [feeling]. Next time we make a plan and you commit to it, I want you show up no matter what [need]."

"I'm not a child." This may seem like an observation of the facts when you say it to a parent who wants you home by 10 p.m., but it's contaminated shorthand for "I'm almost eighteen [observation]. That's old enough to stay out until midnight once in a while [thought]. I'll feel embarrassed and resentful if I have to leave in the middle of my friends' movie marathon [feeling]. I want to stay out until midnight this time [need]."

"What's your problem?" This probably isn't a simple question in many situations. Imagine it's said to a lead singer of a band who's chronically late to rehearsals and shows up high most of the time. A whole message might be "We all usually show up on time, and you don't. Plus, you're often blazed [observation]. It makes me think you don't take the band seriously or have any consideration for the rest of us [thought]. It makes me sad and frustrated [feeling]. We want you here by six on Tuesday, ready to play [need]."

Often the difference between a simple statement of fact and a contaminated message is not the words themselves, but the tone of voice or body language. For example, "I don't care" can be the simple truth. But if it's said in a loud, scathing tone of voice, it could mean "I hate you." Alternatively, if it's said in a monotone without eye contact, it could mean "Leave me alone."

∗ kelly ∗ My brother Eric has had this plaid flannel shirt for a few years now and it's getting worn-out. My mom is sick of him always wearing the shirt, and the two of them often get into arguments about it. When she sees him by the door, ready to go out to dinner, she usually says something like "Can you get dressed for dinner?" He then responds, "This is what I'm wearing." She always groans in disapproval. Here's how she could decontaminate this message by separating her observations, thoughts, feelings, and needs:

"You're wearing that old shirt that I've been asking you to give away [observation]. I think it's too worn and dingy-looking to wear out to a restaurant [thought]. I feel frustrated that you continue to wear it even though it bothers me [feeling]. I would really appreciate it if you wore one of your newer shirts [need]."

Preparing Your Message

Delivering whole messages and avoiding partial or contaminated messages requires three key skills: self-awareness, considering your audience, and being aware of the time and place. In other words, you need self-awareness, other awareness, and place awareness.

Self-Awareness

First, focus on yourself: What are you observing, thinking, and feeling, and what do you need? What's the purpose of your communication? Do your words, body language, and tone of voice match that purpose? What are you most afraid to say? What do you most need to communicate? What's the hardest part of your message to get across?

When you want to convey an important message, it's a good idea to mentally rehearse a few times to get the facts and your thoughts, feelings, and needs straight in your mind. Separate the facts you know to be true from your thoughts, opinions, or theories. Get in touch with your emotions and find a way to express them clearly and honestly. Also come up with a non-threatening way to express your needs.

Exercise: Assessing Your Self-Awareness in Conversation

Bring to mind a recent conversation, then consider how much self-awareness you brought to sharing your message. In your journal, take some time to record the observations, thoughts, feelings, and needs you communicated. You may find it helpful to reflect on the questions in the preceding section on self-awareness to help you bring new insight to the situation.

Other Awareness

Before you start talking, consider your audience. Make sure that others are paying attention and that they're in a receptive mood. For example, if a friend has just failed algebra for the second time, this isn't a good time to complain about getting a C in English. Be sure to notice whether others are rushed, upset, preoccupied, angry, and so on, and be prepared to adjust your message and communicate later if they don't seem receptive.

Other awareness continues as you're talking. Attend to people's facial expressions, body language, and tone of voice, in addition to what they actually say. Are they making eye contact, leaning forward, asking questions, and giving feedback? Or are they distracted, perhaps glancing at their phone or people nearby?

Place Awareness

It's best to talk about important things when you and the other person are alone, away from distractions, and unlikely to be interrupted. It's especially important to pick a place where you won't be overheard. Knowing that others might overhear often causes people to veil their meanings, leave out emotions, tone down their needs, and otherwise distort their message so that it's innocuous and sanitized for public consumption. Find a place that's private, physically comfortable, and quiet, where you won't be interrupted and where there are few distractions.

✱ kelly ✱ Recently, I was hanging out with a group of my friends, and my friend Sam made a snide comment directed toward me. I felt the urge to talk with him about it right then, but I stopped myself and thought about the situation. He was bringing up an issue between the two of us in front of a larger group of people, but a social gathering isn't the appropriate environment for a serious conversation. Even though I wanted to address the issue, I knew the conversation would be more productive if I waited until we were alone. The bottom line? Make sure the setting is appropriate for what you're trying to communicate.

Using Whole Messages to Navigate Difficult Situations

By now, you're probably starting to see how important whole messages are. Shortly, we'll provide detailed guidelines for crafting whole messages. But first, let's take a look at how helpful whole messages are in situations that are difficult to navigate. We'll provide two real-life examples of partial messages, followed by a more effective whole message. In each case, you can clearly see how the whole message clears up the communication and helps prevent misunderstandings and hurt feelings.

Sophie's Story

Sophie is telling her dad that she dropped out of the debate club. She's shy, and she felt excluded by the older kids in the club, who have lots of debate experience and are already good friends with each other. After trying the debate club, Sophie realized that she'd rather join the student council. Sophie's dad was on the debate team when he was in high school, and she thinks he'll be disappointed in her. Sophie omits all of this information and only tells her dad, "The debaters act superior to everyone else. Everybody at school thinks so."

Now, let's look at how Sophie could increase the effectiveness of her communication with a whole message: "Dad, I thought debate would be fun, so I gave it a try. I really enjoyed debating, but I thought some of the club members were unfriendly and too competitive. And I didn't feel connected to any of the people. It makes me sad to not follow the family tradition and do debate, but I really like the idea of being a member of the student council. This way I can try spending time with a different group of people and still be involved with an important aspect of the school."

As you can see, Sophie's whole message includes her observations, thoughts, feelings, and needs.

Chris's Story

Chris is turning eighteen next week. His girlfriend, Sarah, offered to cook him a family dinner at her house to celebrate, but Chris would rather go out for a casual dinner with just Sarah.

Her parents' scrutiny makes him anxious, and her younger siblings are noisy and annoying. When Sarah asks him again which night he's available to come over and celebrate, Chris says in an irritated tone, "I don't really know what my plans are. I'll let you know when I do."

Here's how Chris could increase the effectiveness of his communication with a whole message: "Dinner at your house would be with four other people. I think your parents can't help grilling me about school and my college plans, and your brothers compete for my attention. I feel under pressure to perform—to be the perfect boyfriend. I'd rather have a birthday dinner with just you, even if it's only burgers or pizza."

Again, Chris's whole message includes his observations, thoughts, feelings, and needs.

Exercise: Crafting Your Own Whole Messages

Communicating with whole messages, rather than partial or contaminated messages, is a skill that will improve with practice. So think of a difficult situation you've dealt with recently, perhaps along the lines of the preceding examples. Then write out a whole message you could have used to express yourself, incorporating all four components: observations, thoughts, feelings, and needs.

With practice, using whole messages will become a habit. It will get easier, and eventually almost automatic, to separate what you want to say into observations, thoughts, feelings, and needs. You'll also start to notice when you're tempted to use partial messages, perhaps leaving out your emotions or needs, or contaminated messages, disguising negative feelings as facts or thoughts. With time, you'll also be able to identify what you know, think, feel, and need much more quickly and accurately.

Guidelines for Effective Expression

Using whole messages will go a long way toward improving and deepening your communication with others. Beyond that, bringing certain qualities to your statements will make them even more effective. Ultimately, you'll want to strive for statements that are direct, immediate, clear, straight, and supportive. In the following sections, we'll dive deeper into each of those attributes.

Be Direct

Communicating directly means not making any assumptions. Don't assume that others already know what you think, feel, want, or need. Tell them, directly.

Here are a couple of examples to show you how assumptions can complicate communication in important relationships.

Ian was struggling in school, and his mom was concerned about his grades. She stayed on top of him about it, checking in with him about his assignments every night, until his grades started to improve. Then she stopped bringing up the topic so often, assuming that Ian knew how happy she was. Meanwhile, Ian felt resentful and depressed because his mom didn't tell him how proud she was of his hard work.

Alexander gave Joelle a sweatshirt that she often borrowed from him when they were hanging out after class and it cooled down in the late afternoon. Alexander felt like he was expressing his interest and affection by giving Joelle his sweatshirt, but he didn't come right out and say he liked her; he assumed it was obvious from his gesture. Meanwhile, Joelle came to the conclusion that she'd never be more than Alexander's friend, so she started spending time with another guy who was more direct about his feelings.

In these kinds of situations, people suffer unnecessarily because they don't say directly what they feel or need. They assume others can read their mind or somehow figure out what they're thinking. Of course, no one can truly read other people's minds. The only thing you can safely assume is that the people in your life can't be sure what you want or need unless you tell them directly.

The most common cause of indirect communication is fear. You may have an opinion, feeling, or need that you know you should share with a certain person, but feel afraid to say anything directly. In these cases, people often resort to being indirect, hinting at their opinion or telling a third party in hopes that the message will eventually get to the person they're afraid to talk to directly.

* **kelly** * Sometimes I find it hard to express how I feel directly, especially if it involves an awkward situation. I became close with a coworker who's a few years older than I am. She was fun to spend time with, and she even offered me advice a few times. I felt uncomfortable though, because she started talking down to me, calling me "little nugget" and saying things like "Aw, you'll figure

it out. There's still so much for you to learn!" When she said these things, I gave her hints to show her that I didn't like being addressed that way. Ultimately, though, that strategy didn't clearly communicate to her how I was feeling. I continued to be frustrated until I told her directly how her comments made me feel.

Communicate Immediately

It generally isn't a good idea to brood over painful feelings, such as anger or hurt. Delaying communication tends to amplify negative feelings, allowing them to build up and grow out of proportion. Anger smolders until you lash out. Frustration becomes chronic bitterness. Sometimes suppressed irritation or hurt feelings come out later in passive, indirect ways.

There are two main advantages to immediate communication. First, people can learn what you want from them and adjust their behavior accordingly if they choose. Second, your close relationships will grow in intimacy and intensity because conflicts won't escalate and you won't let opportunities to express your feelings pass.

Communicate Clearly

Clear messages are a refinement of whole messages. In addition to including observations, thoughts, feelings, and needs, they also are accurate and precise. They aren't vague, generalized, or abstract, nor are they expressed with a lot of slang or jargon or laden with unrelated information. They also aren't disguised as questions. Here are some tips for making your statements clear.

Don't ask questions when you need to make a statement. Here are some examples that illustrate why such questions are ineffective:

* A mother asks her son, "Why do you have to go out for track?" A more accurate statement would have reflected her feelings and voiced her concerns, for example, "I'm worried that you won't have enough time for schoolwork if you're on another sports team." Her son won't get this message from her question.

* A daughter asks her mom, "Why do we have to go visit Grandpa tonight?" This question fails to address her needs, which would have been better expressed with a statement like "I've been at a tournament all day, and I'm feeling really tired. Can we see Grandpa another night this week?"

* A girl asks her cousin, "Are you wearing *that* to the party?" She could have been more helpful to her cousin if she'd expressed her opinion: "Maybe you should wear the green top. It's a little more casual and it would make your eyes stand out."

Keep your messages congruent. By "congruent," we mean that your tone of voice, facial expression, gestures, and posture should match the content of what you're saying. Incongruence confuses people because your words say one thing and your body says another. The contradiction may not even register with others, but they still feel that something about your communication isn't quite on target. It turns others off and can create mistrust and misunderstanding. So if, for example, you're excited to see your brother when he's home from college, show him that you'd like to spend time together by making eye contact and being engaged when you're talking to him.

Avoid double messages. Double messages are like kissing someone and hitting them at the same time. Here's an example: Evan says to Julia, "I want to take you to the hockey game because I definitely want to hang out. But it'll be just a bunch of guys commenting on the game and cracking jokes. You don't know anything about the players, so you'll just be bored." While the first part of his message seems to say that Julia is welcome to come, the rest of the statement makes it fairly obvious that he doesn't want her there and would rather just watch the hockey game with his friends.

Focus on one thing at a time. Resist the temptation to change the subject or drag unrelated topics or information into a discussion. If you're talking to your sister about how you'd appreciate her help with unpacking the groceries, it's not the time to bring up how messy she leaves the bathroom. Stick with the current topic; don't obscure it with unrelated information.

Be Straight

A straight message is one where the true intention and the stated intention are the same. Disguised intentions and hidden agendas destroy intimacy because they manipulate people instead of communicating with them. To determine whether you're delivering a straight message, ask yourself, "Why am I saying this to this person? Do I want the person to hear my real reason for saying it, or am I trying to pass it off as something else?" Ask yourself what your true motivation is.

Hidden agendas are covered in the next chapter. They mostly arise out of a need to appear smart, good, in control, strong, and so on. In other words, people often use hidden agendas in an attempt to make themselves look better. For example, if you're trying to show that you're cool, you might talk at length about a cult band's newest album or a cutting-edge indie film that just came out, without a genuine intent to share information.

Being straight also involves telling the truth and not misrepresenting your emotions. For example, if you go to a party with a friend and want to leave because you're feeling awkward and left out, you'd tell that to your friend, rather than making up an excuse like you're tired and have to get up early the next morning. Another example is not fishing for compliments by putting yourself down. Telling lies, even small, social "white" lies, puts distance between you and others. It isolates you and keeps others—and even you—from having a clear idea of what you feel and need.

Be Supportive

Being supportive means having positive motivations and expressing your message in such a way that it won't be received as critical, sarcastic, hostile, or demanding. When you're supportive, your purpose is to genuinely communicate, not to compete, blame, or compare yourself to the other person. Unsupportive messages come from a desire to win, be right, be better, or get your way regardless of the consequences. Ask yourself, "Do I want to communicate in a supportive and positive way, or am I motivated by something else, like winning or the need to be right?" When you want to be supportive, be sure to avoid the following common mistakes.

Using global labels, especially negative ones. Using negative labels is totally unsupportive. It's also one way to guarantee that people you're talking with will feel put down and stop listening to you. If you have to use negative terms, apply them to a person's behavior, not to the person as a whole. For example, instead of saying, "You're selfish," identify the selfish behavior and take responsibility for your opinion: "When you took all the credit, I thought that was a selfish thing to do."

Using sarcasm. While it may seem humorous, sarcasm can communicate that you don't care about others, particularly if they don't know you well. This is clearly unsupportive. In addition, it often indicates that some self-awareness may be in order, since sarcasm can be a way of disguising anger or hurt feelings.

✻ **kelly** ✻ I think sarcasm can be hilarious in conversation with my friends, but I try to remind myself that there are distinct times and places for it. Also, I've noticed that I can make sarcastic jokes to a friend one day and it goes okay, but the next day the same person will be hurt and offended by a similar comment. Make sure your sarcastic comments aren't coming from a place of anger or judgment—your friends will probably be able to tell if they are.

Digging up the past. Try to stick to current events. Spending time rehashing past mistakes and conflicts will only obscure whatever problems you may need to solve in the present. It can also make others feel attacked, which is clearly unsupportive.

Making negative comparisons. Assessing somebody negatively in comparison to someone else puts them immediately on the defensive. That makes it hard for people to hear anything else you say and also makes them unlikely to agree with you or do what you're requesting. These kinds of comparisons can show up in slightly tricky ways. An example of this would be "Nobody else had an issue with me canceling the plan at the last minute."

Sending judgmental you-messages. Avoid phrasing messages in ways that blame the other person. Here are some examples: "You never give me a chance." "You weren't there when I needed you." "You're so selfish and clueless." Instead, use I-messages to express your feelings and needs. Here's how you can do that with those same three examples: "I want you to trust me." "When I'm on my own I feel scared and lonely." "I need you to do your share around here." Note that just using the word "I" isn't enough; you also need to avoid being accusatory and critical. For example, "I need you to not be so messy" isn't supportive. Stay clear about your message and intent, and make sure you aren't using I-messages to communicate criticism.

Threats. It's probably pretty obvious that threats aren't supportive. Plus, if you threaten to leave, quit, or tell on someone, all communication stops, so it's self-defeating if you have an important message to convey.

Putting It All Together

When you express yourself clearly and completely, your relationships improve. You'll be closer to your friends, your parents will be more understanding, your siblings will be more cooperative, and your teachers or bosses will be more supportive. It's well worth devoting some practice to the skills in this chapter so you can clearly and consistently express what you observe, think, feel, and need in whole messages, without hostility, defensiveness, or manipulation.

chapter 4

Recognizing Hidden Agendas

There are people who always seem to be saying the same thing. Every comment, every complaint, and every story seems to have the same message: how smart they are, how tough they are, what victims they are, how messed up everyone else is, and so on. It gets annoying after a while because that's all you hear—the same hidden agenda.

People use hidden agendas for a reason: these messages, delivered over and over, protect them. Always talking about how good or smart or blameless they are, or how screwed up others are, protects their sense of self-worth.

Yet people also use messages about how messed up, helpless, or fragile they are to protect themselves. Because of these messages, no one expects them to succeed or give much. And sometimes these messages lead others to support them or take care of them—at least for a while.

So on the one hand, hidden agendas can be very successful. They can protect self-esteem or garner a lot of support. But on the other hand, they're often quite costly. They can alienate others and make it hard to have friendships that are close and genuine.

The Eight Hidden Agendas

There are eight common hidden agendas that can hurt relationships, and the more they're used, the more damaging they become. In the sections that follow, we'll take a close look at each of these eight agendas and help you learn to recognize them in yourself and others.

"I'm Good"

The "I'm good" agenda is focused on unrelenting self-praise. People with this agenda can do no wrong. They're the hero of every story and portray themselves as generous, caring, and wise. They don't share about their mistakes, struggles, fears, and moments of uncertainty. All they talk about is their successes, good choices, and how much everybody likes them.

The function of this agenda is to protect self-esteem. Only selected parts of these people's identity are seen. It's hard to trust them or feel close to them because you don't really know them.

Exercise: Considering the Downsides of the "I'm Good" Agenda

Think of people you know who use the "I'm good" agenda. How does hearing this message over and over make you feel? Perhaps bored, distrustful, irritated, or put off? Do you wish they could just be real? Think about how this agenda affects you, then describe your feelings in your journal.

Now here's what could be the hard part: Are there situations or relationships where you use the "I'm good" agenda? Try to be honest. Think about friends and family. Think about situations like parties, sports, school activities, dating, or even dinner at home or just hanging out. Does the "I'm good" agenda creep in anywhere? Are you using it in certain relationships or situations where it might be a problem? If so, spend some time writing about this in your journal. Now consider this possibility: How you feel when listening to the "I'm good" agenda may be how others react to you when you slip into this mode.

"I'm Good (But Others Aren't)"

In this hidden agenda, people try to prove their worth by putting others down. Every story or complaint paints someone else as stupid, selfish, incompetent, boring, mean, and so forth. Here are a couple of examples of how this might show up in conversation: "I'm always there for her when she needs something. But when I'm down, forget it. She blows me off." "There are people who work hard and try hard on this team, like me, but he isn't one of them."

The function of this agenda is also to boost self-esteem. And, admittedly, sometimes it feels good to sit around and agree about how messed up somebody is. But if that's all a friend talks about, it can get boring. You may wonder if there's anything else your friend cares about and start to wish he or she was interested in something other than people's flaws. Plus, it's hard to trust people who are always putting others down.

Exercise: Considering the Downsides of the "I'm Good (But Others Aren't)" Agenda

Do you know people who frequently use the agenda "I'm good (but others aren't)"? How does this message affect you? Is it enjoyable, or are you sometimes uncomfortable? Do you worry that they might be directing some criticism your way when you aren't around? Do you wish sometimes that conversations with these people could be about something besides criticizing others? Think about how this agenda affects you, then describe your feelings in your journal.

Now examine whether this hidden agenda might be an issue for you. Everybody does this sometimes, but are there people with whom you use this agenda a lot? If so, consider whether these people may feel the same way you do when you encounter this hidden agenda in others.

"You're Good (But I'm Not)"

The agenda "You're good (but I'm not)" is basically flattery, but with the twist that people put themselves down in the process: "You're so good at dancing. I can barely walk without tripping over my own feet." "I can't add two and two, but you're totally getting this trigonometry stuff."

People sometimes take this one-down position in an attempt to get compliments, reassurance, or favors. And though it may seem counterintuitive, sometimes it's a strategy to ward off anger or rejection when they feel that others have failed them or screwed up. The message "You're wonderful, but I'm awful" is designed to defuse their disappointment and reboot the friendship.

The trouble is, this kind of manipulation is pretty transparent. And people often resent flattery when it's done for the purpose of getting favors, compliments, or forgiveness.

* **kelly** * When I'm trying to connect with someone, I sometimes fall into the "You're good (but I'm not)" agenda. For example, I might say something like "Wow, I can't believe you stopped yourself from eating another cupcake! You're so disciplined. I have no self-control. Yesterday, I ate a whole pint of ice cream." Flattering others seems like a good way to get them to like me and want to spend more time together. But when I say those kinds of things, it distorts communication because others feel like they have to give a compliment in return, like "But you're the one who's always at the gym!"

Exercise: Considering the Downsides of the "You're Good (But I'm Not)" Agenda

Do you know people who put out the "You're good (but I'm not)" message? How do you feel when you hear it? Flattered? Distrustful? Resentful? Do you wonder what they want or where the situation is leading? Describe your reactions in your journal.

Now consider whether you sometimes send this message to people. Are there specific relationships and situations where you tend to do it? What are you hoping for when you do this? Does it work? How do others react? How do you think they might feel? Consider all of these questions and write your answers in your journal.

"I Suffer; I'm Helpless"

The message "I suffer; I'm helpless" centers around being in pain. With people who have this hidden agenda, conversations tend to be about the misfortunes they've suffered or how they've been treated unfairly or abused. Their core experience is of being stuck, with no way out. At first you may feel sympathetic, but after a while you'll probably want to hear something different than how awful everything is. On top of this, if you offer help or advice, these people often say, "Yes, but..." or "I'd like to do that, but I can't because..."

The purpose of the "I suffer; I'm helpless" agenda is to win support and sympathy and get you on that person's side. But it can damage relationships. Over time, it becomes hard to just hear about pain, without any potential for solutions or change. And you may get frustrated at always hearing "Yes, but..." when you offer help. People often distance themselves from friends who seem to have endless problems that can't be solved.

Exercise: Considering the Downsides of the "I Suffer; I'm Helpless" Agenda

Think of the people you know who use the agenda "I suffer; I'm helpless." Does it make you feel closer to them? Do you feel sympathetic and caring? After a while, do you find yourself feeling tired and disengaged? Do you sometimes feel alienated by how stuck and unable to change they seem? Describe your reactions in your journal.

Now consider whether there are relationships or situations where you slip into this agenda yourself. If so, what are you hoping for when you do that? Do these relationships end up feeling closer and more caring, or do people sometimes back away? Spend some time reflecting on these questions and writing about this in your journal.

"I'm Blameless"

A hidden agenda of "I'm blameless" serves as a refuge when things go wrong. It's how people try to cover up or excuse their mistakes. This agenda often shows up in friendships where one person keeps screwing up. Here are a few examples of how it might sound: "I had no idea you'd be hurt when I said I didn't like your hair. You always say you want to know how you look." "I didn't talk trash about you at the party. I was just trying to explain why you're always late." "I couldn't pick you up because my car was out of gas and I didn't have any money left on my debit card."

In other words, the fault always lies elsewhere: "If my parents hadn't put me in this crappy school, I'd be fine." Another form of this agenda is "Look what you made me do." In this variation, people say things like "You told me to ask her out, but she acted like I had rabies. Nice going."

We all make excuses sometimes, but "I'm blameless" is a lifestyle—a way of always avoiding responsibility. It may shield people from their own poor choices and some pain, but it also prevents them from learning from their mistakes. And in the long run, it creates distrust and resentment in others.

> **✳ kelly ✳** When I was younger, I was so afraid of having my behavior met with disapproval or punishment that I often blamed my actions on the situation or circumstance. For example, if I didn't take the dogs for a walk like I was supposed to, I would mention how rainy and muddy it had been that afternoon and that the dogs would have gotten dirty if I'd taken them out. But the truth was that I just didn't feel like doing it. In my mind, doing this absolved me of any blame or responsibility.

Exercise: Considering the Downsides of the "I'm Blameless" Agenda

Do you know people who rely on the "I'm blameless" agenda? When people make excuses instead of taking responsibility for their actions, how does that make you feel? Does it affect your level of trust? And over time, does it tend to make you feel closer to or more distant from these people? Describe your reactions to this agenda in your journal.

Now consider whether there are any situations or relationships where you use this agenda. If so, how do you think it affects those relationships? Based on your own reactions to this agenda, how do you think others feel when you use it? Spend some time writing about this in your journal.

"I'm Fragile"

When people use the "I'm fragile" agenda, their words, tone, or gestures indicate that they're too vulnerable to hear what you want to say. They send the message that it would be too upsetting or overwhelming to know what's going on for you. This agenda can show up in statements like "Please don't say that," "I can't take it when you look at me like that," "After everything I've been through, I can't deal with that," or "Can't you tell that I'm not in the mood to discuss that right now?"

Ultimately, "I'm fragile" puts a stop to communication, and then issues and problems never get resolved. People who use this agenda may protect themselves from being hurt temporarily. But their relationships deteriorate because conflicts and painful feelings never get processed.

Exercise: Considering the Downsides of the "I'm Fragile" Agenda

Do any of the people in your life use the "I'm fragile" agenda when you want to talk something out or try to share something you're going through? How do you react when that happens? Do you feel guilty for upsetting them? Do you feel worried, frustrated, or angry? Take some time to write about your reactions in your journal.

Now consider whether you ever use this agenda. If so, how has it affected your relationships? Was the other person concerned about you? Did the other person draw closer or pull away? Take some time to write about this in your journal too.

"I'm Tough"

The "I'm tough" agenda is a mask people use to hide vulnerability. They let everyone know they carry a big load in life, facing a lot of stress and huge challenges, but because of their agenda of appearing tough and invulnerable, they never show any reaction. If they're in pain, no one sees it. And if you push them, trying to lift the mask to see what's underneath, they get angry. The message is "Don't mess with me," "I have nothing to give you," or "You can't know me, so don't try."

The main purpose of this agenda is to ward off or hide pain and prevent anyone from getting close enough to hurt the person. The problem is that this means all relationships stay distant; there's no intimacy. The "I'm tough" agenda sometimes makes people seem intriguing, causing others to hope to be the one who finally penetrates the wall. But these people have their masks on tight, so others can devote years to the relationship and never really get to know them.

Exercise: Considering the Downsides of the "I'm Tough" Agenda

Do you know people who communicate with this agenda? Does it make you interested or attracted? Or does it make you feel scared of them, angry, put off, or frustrated that you can't get close? Whatever reactions you may have, spend some time writing about this in your journal.

Now consider whether you tend to play it tough in certain situations or relationships. If so, how does this work for you? Do you feel safer and less vulnerable? Do you feel more unseen and alone? Are people drawn to you, or do they tend to stay away? The agenda has advantages and disadvantages. Is it worth what it may be costing you? Spend some time reflecting on these questions and writing your answers in your journal.

"I Know It All"

People with the "I know it all" agenda lecture, advise, and have answers for everything. Their opinions are strong and seldom influenced by others. If you disagree with them, they tend to make you feel stupid. Their knowledge sometimes impresses, but after a while it feels oppressive. It seems like there's no room for your thoughts or beliefs.

The function of this agenda is to ward off feelings of shame or inadequacy. And it works pretty well—for a while. The problem is, people become annoyed when their opinions are always discounted, and they withdraw when they're made to feel stupid or wrong.

While this agenda is often motivated by a desire to get positive attention and admiration from others, it can end up being more isolating than helpful. And as with the other hidden agendas, although it protects, it also limits the growth and depth of relationships.

Exercise: Considering the Downsides of the "I Know It All" Agenda

How do you feel when you encounter people with the "I know it all" agenda? Are you drawn to them because they seem smart? Are you put off by their tendency to lecture when communicating? Do you feel stupid or irritated around them? Take some time to describe your reactions in your journal.

You're probably well aware of it if you fall into this agenda. People tend to complain about it. And they probably feel some of the same reactions you have when you interact with someone who has this agenda. If you feel this agenda is an issue for you, spend some time writing about this and how it affects your relationships.

Do the Opposite

Now that you're familiar with those common hidden agendas, you have a pretty good idea of why it's worthwhile to work on changing any agenda that you're prone to. All of them present obstacles to forming close, trusting, supportive relationships. In general, all of these agendas lead to the same four issues:

* They keep people from feeling close to you.

* They manipulate others to see you in ways that aren't entirely accurate.

* They make it hard to connect with people and find new friends.

* They leave you feeling alone because people don't really know you.

If you want to change any of these communication styles, you can definitely do it. We recommend the following three-step process, which we'll describe in detail below:

1. Start practicing opposite action in specific situations.

2. Learn to recognize your hidden agendas when they show up.

3. Practice opposite action on the fly, whenever you notice hidden agendas showing up.

Step 1. Practice Opposite Action in Specific Situations

In this step, you'll identify situations where you tend to use hidden agendas and then come up with a plan for communicating differently—in exactly the opposite way, in fact—in those circumstances. Here are some examples to give you an idea of how you might do this.

Agenda: "I'm good."

Opposite action: Reveal one or two things you struggle with and would like to change.

Agenda: "I'm good (but others aren't)."

Opposite action: Identify several things you can praise or appreciate in others—without bragging about yourself.

Agenda: "You're good (but I'm not)."

Opposite action: Say something positive about both yourself and the other person. For example, you might talk about a strength the two of you share.

Agenda: "I suffer; I'm helpless."

Opposite action: Choose to talk about something you've overcome or achieved in the face of difficulty. Share one of your strengths.

Agenda: "I'm blameless."

Opposite action: The next time you make a mistake, acknowledge it. Try saying something like "I could have done better with that. It's something I want to work on."

Agenda: "I'm fragile."

Opposite action: Commit to really listening to the other person's experience—even if it's painful. Acknowledge in your own words what the other person says.

Agenda: "I'm tough."

Opposite action: Plan to share one small vulnerability—something a bit painful that you've been dealing with.

Agenda: "I know it all."

Opposite action: Plan to listen and ask questions about the other person's opinion or experience. Find out where the other person is coming from before saying what you know or believe.

Exercise: Practicing Doing the Opposite

Now that you have an idea of how opposite action works, you can give it a try yourself. Choose the hidden agenda you most want to change, then think of a few situations in which that agenda tends to show up. In those situations, what, specifically, do you communicate? Be clear about exactly what you say.

Now make a plan to do the exact opposite, and record it in your journal. Once you've decided on the specifics of how you'll do the opposite, make a commitment to follow through in each of the situations you identified. Sometimes it helps to share your plans with a trusted friend so that person can provide support and reminders about your effort to change.

Step 2. Recognize Your Hidden Agendas

Hidden agendas tend to show up in some typical ways. If you can learn to spot them when they arise, you'll be in a better position to choose to respond differently, even when you don't have an advance plan for engaging in opposite action. To give you an idea of the kinds of signals you're looking for, here are a few examples.

Agenda: "I'm good."

Signals: Bragging. This can show up as trying to impress others or presenting yourself as perfect.

Agenda: "I'm good (but other aren't)."

Signals: Criticizing others and complaining about them. This might be a reaction to not feeling good about yourself or your performance in a particular situation, or it could be a way to distract others from recognizing something about you that you're sensitive about.

Agenda: "You're good (but I'm not)."

Signals: Flattering others and negatively comparing yourself to them. This might be a response to feeling anxious about others liking you.

Agenda: "I suffer; I'm helpless."

Signals: Complaining about how much pain you're in or how stuck you are. This may indicate that you're feeling left out or lonely. It can be a way of trying to get attention.

Agenda: "I'm blameless."

Signals: Making excuses. This can be an attempt to avoid the consequences of making a mistake, including painful feelings associated with disappointing someone.

Agenda: "I'm fragile."

Signals: Telling others you're too upset to listen to them. You may feel anxious or afraid that someone will say something you don't want to hear.

Agenda: "I'm tough."

Signals: Telling stories about how tough you are and how you don't take any crap from anyone. You might feel this way if you've been hurt, or if you feel vulnerable with a particular person or in a specific situation.

Agenda: "I know it all."

Signals: Forcing your opinion on others or lecturing. You may fall into this agenda if you feel the need to take control of another person or a group you're with.

Exercise: Identifying Signals of Your Own Hidden Agendas

If you've been able to engage in opposite action in a few situations, you're ready to work on recognizing old hidden agendas whenever they show up. In your journal, make a short list of signals that indicate you're falling into old patterns with any of the hidden agendas. Then, in the coming days and weeks, be on the lookout for those signals when they show up.

Step 3. Practice Opposite Action on the Fly

Now commit to watching for the signals you identified in the previous exercise. Then, each time you catch yourself, try doing the opposite. (You might want to use your journal to keep track of this.)

To get an idea of how this looks in real life, let's consider Molli, who wants to work on her "I'm fragile" agenda. Friends had complained that she tended to get crushed and refuse to listen when they told her something she didn't like. For example, when her friend Jill told her how withdrawn she seemed at a party, Molli cried and said Jill was making her feel bad about herself. Also, Molli wouldn't tell her boyfriend anything about her family. She said it was too painful. But the truth was, she didn't want him to know about her younger brother, who had been diagnosed with bipolar disorder. And when Molli's older brother came home on leave from the army, she told him she was sad but otherwise wouldn't talk to him.

Molli decided that her opposite action would be staying with conversations, rather than seeming too upset to deal with them. Specifically, she decided to respond differently to Jill, her boyfriend, and her brother, even if that made conversations feel difficult. Then she imagined conversations with each of them and spent some time writing about what she'd say when trying opposite action.

A few days after committing to this strategy, Molli had to practice opposite action on the fly when she learned that Jill was upset with her. Jill complained that she texted Molli all the time but Molli rarely texted back. Molli started to tell Jill that she was too upset about a fight with her boyfriend to talk about it. But she saw right away this was just her old "I'm fragile" agenda. So instead, Molli took a breath and said, "Okay, Jill. What happens when I don't text back? Are you hurt?"

Jill said she was, and in the end they agreed that Molli would text back most of the time—within an hour if she could. This was a totally different outcome than usual with their fights, which typically ended up being about Molli not listening.

Afterward, Molli identified two signals that could clue her in when she started falling into her "I'm fragile" mode. One was anxiety about a conversation, leading to a desire to avoid it. The second was an impulse to complain about how sad, tired, or upset she was. She decided that if either of these signals showed up, she had a choice: be fragile Molli, or fight through her impulse to avoid or complain and instead listen to the other person.

Dealing with the Hidden Agendas of Others

Overcoming your own hidden agendas can be tough. Unfortunately, no matter how successful you are, you'll still have to deal with other people's agendas. When that happens, you can do two things. One is to let it go—if it doesn't bother you too much and it isn't damaging the relationship. But if the agenda affects you emotionally or creates problems in the relationship, you don't have to play along. You can say or do something to stop the agenda and encourage a different form of communication. Here are some examples of how you can do that.

Agenda: "I'm good."

What you can say: "I know you're great. That's why you're my friend. What else can we talk about?"

Agenda: "I'm good (but others aren't)."

What you can say: "I'd rather find the good side of people than what's wrong with them."

Agenda: "You're good (but I'm not)."

What you can say: "Thanks for the compliment, but I don't want it at your expense."

Agenda: "I suffer; I'm helpless."

What you can say: "If you're going to tell me what's wrong, I want to hear what you're going to do about it."

Agenda: "I'm blameless."

What you can say: "Let's not do excuses, okay?"

Agenda: "I'm fragile."

What you can say: "Could you hang in there and let me tell you what's going on with me? I know it's upsetting, but we need to talk about this."

Agenda: "I'm tough."

What you can say: "I know you're strong, but I'd like to hear what's really going on with you."

Agenda: "I know it all."

What you can say: "Either we make room for my opinion, or I want to stop talking about this."

Notice each of these responses stops the conversation cold. The only way people can keep promoting their hidden agendas is if you cooperate. When you don't play along, they have to find a new way to talk to you. You don't have to be mean about it; you just have to be firm.

Here's an example: Joy had a fairly new boyfriend, and since day one she'd complained about him to her friend Siena. It was always the same story: he wanted to hang out with his friends and just have Joy tag along. Joy felt hurt and unappreciated, but she said yes to every invitation. It was a classic "I suffer; I'm helpless" agenda.

After a few weeks of this, Siena was getting pretty frustrated, so she decided to respond differently. The next time they got together, Joy started in on that same, tired line of conversation: "There's nothing I can do. He likes them more. He just wants to fool around with me." Siena held up her hand and said, "Joy, it's been like this from the beginning. Tell me what you're going to do about it, or let's talk about something else."

Joy was quiet for a moment, but she got the point. They decided to watch a movie and forget about boyfriends for a while.

Putting It All Together

Hidden agendas are detrimental to relationships. But thanks to the work you've done in this chapter, you're now in a better position to recognize when you're falling into these agendas. When you do, you can engage in opposite action. This may be difficult at first; breaking habits always is. But in the long run, your relationships will grow stronger and more genuine. And now you're also more likely to notice when you're on the receiving end of one of these agendas. When that happens, you'll probably find yourself feeling put off, irritated, or alienated by the other person's communication style. However, you now have some new strategies to try in these situations. At first it may feel risky to respond in new ways, but in relationships you care about, it's worth the effort.

chapter 5

Understanding Your Beliefs and the Beliefs of Others

Everyone sees the world differently. Your specific experiences and interactions with other people and your environment play a big role in your beliefs and how you view the world. Some of your views may be similar to others', but many aspects of your views and beliefs are unique to you.

Everything about you—your culture and ethnicity, your environment, and the people in your life—has a bearing on your perspective. For example, if you live in a city, your experiences and worldview will differ from those of someone who lives in a small rural town. Specific characteristics can also impact your view of the world, for example, whether you're tall or short, whether you're athletic or artistic, whether you get As or Cs in school, or whether you're an only child or one of five kids in your family.

All of these factors are important, because your view of the world helps you make sense of what's happening around you. It helps you decide what's important, what you need to pay attention to, and what you can safely ignore. Yet it can also be limiting and get in the way of understanding, communicating, and connecting with others, particularly those whose experiences have been very different from yours.

In short, your perspective guides your behavior and determines the choices you make and how you interact with others. And although people often make the assumption that everyone shares their perspective, this isn't the case. Others are always behaving, making choices, and interacting based upon their own perspective and experiences. Often the differences are subtle enough that they don't make communication difficult, but at times people's perspectives and beliefs are enough at odds with yours that you need to clarify your own view or seek clarification from them.

The purpose of this chapter is to offer you skills that will allow you to be open and understanding in your interactions with others. This approach will help you make more diverse, enriching, and meaningful connections in your life. By bringing awareness to the differences between your own beliefs and the beliefs of others, as well as the limitations inherent in all perspectives, you can increase your understanding. As a result, your world will feel more connected and dynamic.

✳ kelly ✳ Even though I spent part of my childhood living in a diverse city, I was surprised by the variety of viewpoints I encountered when I arrived at college. For example, I don't have an intimate connection with traditional religion, so at times the environment of my

Catholic university feels unfamiliar to me. The fact that I don't understand many Catholic traditions can make me feel awkward and uninformed. I also sometimes feel excluded, like I'm not part of a community that has such a presence on campus. Recognizing how my beliefs are different helped me start making an effort to learn about other students' perspectives and belief systems. Having open, inclusive conversations with them about their faith helps me broaden my perspective and allows me to feel more comfortable in my school community.

Using Compassion to Expand Your World

Sometimes people are quick to notice differences between themselves and others. This creates distance. People tend to be attracted to those who are similar to them and feel safer with what's familiar. One way to bridge the distance between yourself and others is compassion, which enhances all social relationships.

Compassion helps us see others as being similar to ourselves. After all, there are a lot of commonalities in our basic human experience. For one, we all suffer. In essence, you practice compassion whenever you recognize other people's suffering and feel a desire to alleviate that suffering. Compassion means seeing that others, no matter what their culture, ethnicity, or other characteristics, are fundamentally like you, and that feelings of inadequacy and disappointment are universal. From this perspective, you're aware that the pain you feel in difficult times is the same pain others feel in difficult times. As a result, they no longer seem to be separate from you.

Exercise: Cultivating Compassion

Think of a situation in which you found yourself making judgments or conclusions based upon limited knowledge about someone's background, culture, ethnicity, or a group the person was part of. Did your judgments create an obstacle to being open to exploring what the two of you might have in common? Did you remain open enough to recognize that there were similarities you overlooked or missed early on? Take some time to write about your experiences in your journal.

The bottom line is that when you bring kindness and openness to your experiences and those of others, you'll feel more connected. However, all of that said, you cannot truly know what others are experiencing unless they share it with you. And even then, their communication may be unclear or vague. That's where clarification, the topic of the next section, comes in.

Using Clarification to Deepen Understanding

In this section, you'll learn how to use clarifying questions to better understand your beliefs, values, and perspectives and those of others. As you'll learn, all perspectives can have limitations or be distorted. We'll explain why this is the case and how you can notice when it's happening, and then give you some techniques for challenging these limitations and distortions.

Instead of assuming you know what other people are talking about, it's important to make an effort to understand their beliefs and perspectives. You have to ask questions to uncover what other people really mean. Don't take even simple words at face value, assuming that your definitions of words like "confused," "happy," or "unfair" are the same as other people's definitions.

One common way communication and relationships get into trouble is when two people use the same words but associate them with different meanings. Terms like "relationship," "love," "fidelity," "right," "wrong," "selfish," "duty," "lonely," and "respect" can mean different things to different people. You can probably see how this could lead to trouble.

There are four particularly common communication habits that tend to obscure people's perspectives and beliefs:

* Omissions

* Vague pronouns

* Vague verbs

* Abstractions and other vague nouns

> **✳ kelly ✳** We've provided examples of each problematic communication habit, along with examples of clarifying questions. These will probably read like stiff, unnatural conversations. I'm sure you don't talk in these ways—and we aren't recommending that you adopt these particular questions. We simply provide them to bring awareness to the problems that can result when people don't ask clarifying questions.

Omissions

Omissions are pretty obvious. People often make incomplete statements that leave out important information. If you aren't aware of this, you may fill in the blanks based on your own beliefs about the world, in which case you could completely misunderstand what the other person is saying. The way to deal with omissions is to resist making automatic assumptions and instead ask simple, straightforward questions. For example, if your roommate says he's upset and leaves it at that, don't assume you know what's making him upset. Ask "About what?" or "About whom?"

Here are some examples of statements with major omissions and questions you can use to clarify them.

Statement: I'm frustrated.

Questions: About what? Who or what is frustrating you?

Statement: I'm in a better mood now.

Questions: Better than what? How is your mood better?

Statement: I need help.

Questions: From whom? What kind of help do you need?

Statement: Jack's the worst.

Questions: The worst what? How is he the worst?

Exercise: Noticing Omissions

Think of a recent experience when you didn't ask for clarification of an omission and it resulted in a misunderstanding or miscommunication. After you come up with an example, write about it in your journal. Describe the exchange. What word or phrase led to the misunderstanding? What would you ask to avoid the misunderstanding? This happens a lot, and it happens to everyone, yet we often don't notice it. One reason is that we're often in such a rush that it seems more efficient to fill in the missing information than ask for clarification.

Vague Pronouns

Using vague pronouns like "it," "that," and "they" is a common cause of confusion and misunderstanding. Without clarification, it can be easy to think these words are standing in for something or someone other than what the speaker intends. Ask questions to make sure you know what a pronoun refers to. Here are some examples.

Statement: It doesn't matter.

Question: What exactly doesn't matter to you?

Statement: They say it's not a good movie.

Question: Who are "they"?

Statement: It's a problem.

Question: What precisely is the problem?

Statement: That sucks.

Question: What sucks?

Exercise: Noticing Vague Pronouns

Now that you're aware of the problem with vague pronouns, you'll probably start to notice a lot of them, in other people's statements and your own. Think of a few examples of times when this happened and write about them in your journal.

Vague Verbs

Although verbs are more specific than pronouns, they too can be vague, especially common verbs that can have many meanings, like "move," "touch," or "see." Some verbs, like "tickle," "yawn," or "blink," are more specific and less prone to misinterpretation. If someone says, "She doesn't really know me," the verb "know" is pretty vague. Does it mean "understand me at a deep emotional level," "possess certain historical facts about me," or "grasp my motivations"? Here are some examples of vague verb statements and questions that can clarify them.

Statement: I grew a lot last year.

Questions: How did you grow? In height? In maturity? In understanding?

Statement: I love this poem.

Questions: What do you love about the poem?

Statement: The music moves me.

Questions: How does it move you? Do you feel something in particular?

Exercise: Clarifying Vague Verbs

Again, take some time to consider recent interactions. Can you identify any conversations that would have been more beneficial or successful if you'd asked a clarifying question when a vague verb was used? If so, write about this in your journal, including any clarifying questions you might have asked in response to the statement.

> ✳ **kelly** ✳ Recently, a friend told me that he'd started dating his ex-girlfriend again. She hadn't treated him well before, so I said I thought he should be careful not to move too quickly. His reply was "She's changed." I didn't know what he meant by that vague verb statement. I wish I'd asked him questions like "Has she changed her

behavior? Has she changed her appearance? What is she doing differently?" How she's changed could make a big difference in whether or not she'll treat him better.

Abstractions and Other Vague Nouns

Abstractions are common words people use all the time to refer to complicated concepts, situations, and circumstances, for example, "relationship," "problem," or "compatibility." They're handy because they have broad meanings and can encapsulate complex things. But that's also what makes them vague and prone to obscuring clear communication.

Many of the common words people use to describe feelings are actually abstractions: "hate," "fear," "sadness," "guilt," "jealousy," and so on. For example, if your mother says she's jealous of you, what does she really mean? Is she envying your youth, or is this just her way of trying to get you to include her in some of your weekend plans? Sometimes you can tell by context, but sometimes you can't. It's usually better to ask questions than to guess.

Say your best friend tells you she feels guilty about lying to her boyfriend. Does that mean she wishes she had told the truth, wishes she hadn't done something she felt she had to lie about, or wishes she'd been able to avoid saying anything? And for her, is that guilt a slightly uncomfortable feeling or something that feels fundamentally wrong? Until you ask, you can't really know.

Another problem with vague nouns is that they can be part of a passive approach, as these examples show: "We need to make a *decision* about our chemistry project" instead of "Let's *decide* which reaction to demonstrate." Or "You know you can count on our support" instead of "We support you." Here are some more examples of statements that use abstractions or vague nouns, along with questions that could clarify them. In this case, we also provide examples of the more precise communication that could result from asking clarifying questions.

Abstract statement: Our relationship is problematic.

Question: How are we relating that seems to be causing you problems?

More precise statement: Whenever we're together, we seem to be fighting. This makes me feel stressed-out in other parts of my life, like sports. I'm distracted and my performance is suffering.

Abstract statement: Nothing at school is going right.

Question: Exactly what kind of things are going wrong at school?

More precise statement: My English teacher told me I need to be more organized in my writing, and it makes me feel like all of my other academic work is bad.

Abstract statement: It's like my life is one big rejection.

Question: Who is rejecting you and how?

More precise statement: I feel like I'm no one's priority. Spending time with me usually seems to be a backup plan for my friends and family, and that makes me feel unwanted.

Abstract statement: Sorry, but I'm not excited about us anymore.

Question: What was exciting then that isn't happening now?

More precise statement: I think we do the same thing every week—go out to dinner and a movie. It seems like my parents have more fun together than we do.

Abstract statement: We need to figure out some solutions.

Question: What problems would you like to solve, and which should we solve first?

More precise statement: I want to talk about our plans for this weekend, and then about the babysitting job.

Exercise: Clarifying Abstractions with Precise Statements

Over the next few days, tune in to conversations and notice when you or others use abstractions and other vague nouns. Then, using the format above, record a few of these statements in your journal, along with clarifying questions and new, more precise statements that could result from this approach.

Challenging Limited Perspectives

Asking for more information about someone else's perspective can go a long way toward clarifying communication, but sometimes you need to go further and identify the limitations of your own perspective or the perspectives of others. Certain language patterns can be useful signals that you're dealing with a limitation, whether your own or someone else's:

* Absolutes

* Implied limits

* Implied values

Absolutes

Absolutes are exaggerations or overgeneralizations. They usually include words such as "always," "never," "everyone," "nobody," "all," or "none," making them extreme and often untrue. They're problematic in communication because they leave little or no room for compromise. This can be frustrating and alienating.

You can challenge absolutes by asking others if they've ever had an experience that contradicts their statement. For example, if someone tells you that you're always late, you can ask, "Can't you think of even one instance when I was on time?" Here are some absolute statements and questions to challenge them.

Absolute statement: He never picks up the check.

Question: Has he ever paid for a meal when you went out?

Absolute statement: She always sides with Alex.

Question: Has she never recognized your side of the argument?

Absolute statement: Nobody cares about me.

Question: I can think of many people who love and care about you. Can we list some together?

Absolute statement: I hate everything.

Question: I don't believe that everything in your life is awful. What are some things that are making you happy these days?

Exercise: Clarifying Absolutes

Over the next few days, notice when you or others make absolute statements. Write a few examples in your journal, along with alternative statements that are more accurate and nuanced.

Implied Limits

Implied limits involve using terms that suggest you or others have no choice—that there's nothing anyone can do. They're expressed with words like "can't," "must," "have to," "should," "ought to," "necessary," or "impossible."

Implied limits fall into two categories: statements containing words like "can't" and "impossible," which support a perspective of the world in which certain options are entirely unavailable; and statements with words like "should" or "ought to," which imply some kind of moral judgment or obligation. "Should" statements can be especially damaging because they indicate that you're a bad person if you break the implied rules.

Many people limit the scope of their lives by not questioning these kinds of implied limits. For example, you might say, "I can't speak in public at all. Even the smallest group makes me feel tongue-tied." With these kinds of statements, you cut yourself off from attempting to go beyond the implied limit. To challenge this kind of statement, pose a what-if question to yourself:

"What would happen if I *did* address a crowd of people, like at a school assembly?" This directs your attention to the future and imagining a situation in which you might speak in a public setting. Or you might ask, "What am I afraid is going to happen if I try to speak in public?" This strategy is likely to turn your focus to the past to examine where your fear comes from.

"Should" statements and other moral judgments can be challenged in the same way: by imagining a hypothetical situation or considering the origin of the rule. For example, if someone says you shouldn't hang out with a certain crowd, you might respond along these lines: "You say I shouldn't hang out with that group of kids at school. What are you afraid might happen if I do?"

Here are some statements with implied limits and sample questions that could be used to challenge them.

Implied limit: I'd like to go, but I can't.

Question: What's stopping you from going?

Implied limit: You shouldn't say things like that about other people.

Question: What will happen if I say things like that?

Implied limit: I have to do what my coach says.

Question: What would happen if you didn't do what she says?

Implied limit: You should apply to a few more colleges.

Question: What do you fear will happen if I don't apply to any other schools?

Exercise: Challenging Implied Limits

Over the next few days, notice when you or others make statements that contain implied limits and write a few examples in your journal. Then challenge them by imagining hypothetical future situations in which the limit doesn't prevent taking a certain action, or by examining the fear associated with the limit and what the origins of that fear may be.

Implied Values

When people make general statements about the world, those statements are typically based on their beliefs and values about what's right and wrong, appropriate and inappropriate, or good and bad. One way to tell when people are communicating implied values is when they use sweeping global labels such as "greedy," "corrupt," or "ridiculous." This language pattern often indicates that a person is unaware that there are other valid perspectives.

One good way to challenge statements that contain implied values is to encourage people to discuss their own values and be open to the reality that other people may have different values, beliefs, and perspectives. For example, if someone says "Romantic comedies are so boring," you can ask, "Who thinks they're so boring?" Here are some statements containing implied values and questions to challenge them.

Implied value: That's completely worthless.

Question: Who's it worthless to?

Implied value: Breaking up was wrong.

Question: Who was it wrong for?

Implied value: Therapy is stupid.

Question: Who is it stupid for?

Implied value: Teachers care about test performance, not learning.

Question: Who thinks they only care about scores?

Implied value: She's just crazy.

Question: By whose standards is she crazy?

Exercise: Challenging Implied Values

Review the preceding examples of statements containing implied values. Then come up with your own questions to challenge them and write them in your journal.

Challenging Distorted Perspectives

When your view of the world is distorted, you can't see many of the opportunities and alternatives open to you. In this way, your experience of what life has to offer becomes impoverished. There are three language patterns that can lead to distortions:

* Cause and effect errors

* Mind reading

* Presuppositions

Cause and Effect Errors

Cause and effect errors result from the belief that one person can cause another person to experience certain emotions or inner states, and that the second person has no choice in how he or she responds. To see how this works, imagine that you're about to go off to college and your best friend says, "Having you move away makes me feel abandoned, and it will ruin my life," implying that your actions are responsible for how she'll feel and the choices she'll make. To challenge this language pattern, you need to ask two questions: Are your actions genuinely responsible for your friend's feelings? And does she actually have no other way of responding to the change? For example, you could say, "What is it that makes you feel abandoned about my leaving for college, and how will my choice to leave ruin your life?" This is a gentle reminder that everybody is responsible for their own feelings. You can follow up with something like "Are you happy for me? Sad I'll be gone?" Below are some statements with cause and effect errors, along with questions to challenge them.

Cause and effect error: You make me so angry.

Questions: How do I make you mad? What am I doing that you get mad about?

Cause and effect error: Your music gives me a headache.

Questions: Did my music actually make your head hurt?

Cause and effect error: Your silence makes me sad.

Questions: What's depressing about my being quiet?

Cause and effect error: Your driving terrifies me.

Questions: What about my driving is scary to you?

Exercise: Challenging Cause and Effect Errors

Over the next few days, notice when you or others make statements that contain cause and effect errors and write a few examples in your journal. Then come up with some questions that could suggest that the speakers are responsible for their own feelings and responses.

Mind Reading

We discussed mind reading briefly in chapter 1, in the section on listening blocks. As a reminder, it happens whenever people assume they know what other people are thinking without clearly communicating with them. Mind reading distorts people's understanding of the world because it involves making assumptions that probably aren't true. This communication problem is caused by the human tendency to project, meaning a person believes others feel, think, behave, and react the same way he or she does. When you project your own reality onto others, you don't get a chance to discover their truth. Another variation on this theme is assuming that others know how you're feeling, and this can cause trouble too.

When you think others may be engaging in mind reading, ask questions like "How do you know that?" and "What makes you think he feels that way?" Of course, you can also ask the same kinds of questions of yourself. Here are some mind reading statements and questions designed to challenge them.

Mind reading statement: My teacher thinks I'm lazy.

Questions: How do you know that? What has your teacher done or said to show you he thinks that?

Mind reading statement: My boyfriend knows how I feel.

Questions: Does he really? How can you be sure?

Mind reading statement: Don't be mad.

Questions: Why do you say I'm mad?

✳ kelly ✳ I get especially frustrated when other people engage in mind reading during serious, emotionally charged conversations. When I'm trying to get an important point across and the other person interrupts me because they think they know where I'm headed, it derails the conversation.

Exercise: Challenging Mind Reading

Recall a recent experience when mind reading interfered with communication, and write about it in your journal. Then come up with some questions that could have been helpful in challenging the mind reader's assumptions.

Presuppositions

Presuppositions are parts of a statement that must be true in order for the whole statement to be valid. Here's an example: In the statement "Since you got so obnoxious at the last party, let's skip this one," the decision to not go to the next party is only valid if you accept being obnoxious at the previous party as a fact. To challenge this statement, you could ask, "How was I obnoxious last time?" Here are some statements containing presuppositions, along with questions to challenge them.

Presupposition: If you really loved me, you'd understand.

Questions Why do you feel like I don't love you?

Presupposition: I'm seriously sick, so I need a doctor's appointment right away.

Question: What are your symptoms?

Presupposition: She has low self-esteem; that's why they push her around.

Question: What makes you feel like she has low self-esteem?

Exercise: Challenging Presuppositions

Think of a recent experience when someone made a statement that involved a presupposition. Record it in your journal, then think about how you'd challenge the statement now that you've seen some examples. Write your new response in your journal.

Apologizing

Using clarifying questions will help you navigate unclear communications that may include omissions, vague pronouns, vague verbs, or abstractions and other vague nouns. Some of the other skills outlined in this chapter will help you challenge absolutes, implied limits, implied values, cause and effect errors, mind reading, and presuppositions. But even with practice in all of these skills, you'll probably still sometimes have difficult communications due to misunderstandings. Consider what your role was in any misunderstandings and then, if appropriate, offer a sincere apology.

Everyone appreciates an apology when they've been hurt. Just be aware that the phrasing of an apology is important. It must be heartfelt on your part, and it must feel sincere to the other person. It's crucial to convey that you understand that what you said or did hurt the other person's feelings. Phrase your apology in a way that indicates you're taking responsibility for your words and actions and not blaming the other person for his or her response. "I'm sorry that your feelings are hurt" won't cut it because it doesn't indicate that you're taking responsibility. Instead, you might say, "I'm sorry that I said something that hurt your feelings." Apologizing well takes practice, but it's worth the effort. This is an important skill for making connections and keeping relationships strong.

Putting It All Together

Your perspective, beliefs, and values shape who you are as an individual. As you mature, it's important to be open to other perspectives; that way your beliefs and values can grow with you. So pursue interactions and relationships that expand your world, and be compassionate in these conversations.

The clarifying techniques you've learned in this chapter can be extremely helpful, but don't use them all the time. Challenging every vague statement you hear in casual conversation would be incredibly annoying. Use these techniques when you hear someone you care about say something that's unclear, confusing, or obviously the result of a limiting perspective.

How do you know when a speaker's statement needs to be clarified? The best sign is if you feel puzzled—if what's said is confusing, seems incomplete, or just feels wrong. At those times, clarification will prevent you from jumping to conclusions and help you grasp what the speaker really means. As a bonus, seeking to understand others' perspectives will enrich your understanding of the world.

Finally, when you use these clarifying techniques, be cautious and gentle. Challenging someone's perspective can seem hostile, so approach clarification with an attitude of sincere interest and curiosity, not aggression. Most importantly, be open to challenging and expanding your own perspective on the world, including your beliefs and values.

chapter 6

Assertive Communication

Assertiveness is expressing yourself clearly—your feelings, thoughts and wishes—without offending or violating others. It isn't a personality trait that you're born with; it's a skill you can develop. That said, your temperament and the communication styles your parents modeled probably influenced your communication style. As you read this chapter, you may recognize that you tend to use a particular communication style most of the time, or that your style varies depending upon the person you're interacting with and the circumstances. For example, you might notice that your communication style at home is influenced by the ways in which your family communicates.

Not every situation requires assertive communication, but once you learn this skill, you'll probably find yourself communicating assertively, rather than passively or aggressively, most of the time. Part of learning to be assertive is being able to recognize and choose when and where this communication style is helpful. To make that decision, you need to have a good understanding of the three main communication styles, so let's start there.

The Three Main Communication Styles

The first step in assertiveness training is learning the three primary styles of communicating—passive, aggressive, and assertive—and which situations each is best suited to. Everyone uses all three styles, and everyone has been on the receiving end of all three. So as you read through the descriptions of these styles, try to come up with your own real-life examples of each.

Passive

When you use a passive style of communication, you're relying on the other person to read your mind—or try to—because you aren't directly expressing your feelings, thoughts, or wishes. Your communication is indirect. You may try to communicate how you're feeling or what you want through body language (slumped posture, lowered head, crossed arms) or facial expressions (frowning, grimacing, making little or no eye contact). You may pout, cry, or whisper under your breath.

When you use a passive style, you're probably subordinating your needs to others or relying on others to figure those needs out. When someone asks you to do something you don't want to do, you're likely to do it or make an excuse rather than say no. If you do speak up about your needs, you probably qualify what you say with statements like "If it's no trouble…," "I really shouldn't be saying this…," "You probably know better than I do…," or "I'm not really sure but…" In short, you may find it difficult to make requests or to give an honest answer when a request is made of you.

Other signs of a passive style are rambling, being vague, finding yourself at a loss for words, or making frequent use of phrases like "I mean" and "you know." Whether you're aware of it or not, you're hoping that the other person will figure out what you're feeling, needing, or wishing. A passive style turns communication into a guessing game.

Aggressive

In contrast, there's no guessing involved when someone communicates with an aggressive style. If you're using this style, you're letting others know exactly how you're feeling, what you're thinking, and what you want. Unfortunately, this information is delivered in ways that violate others' rights or hurt their feelings. With an aggressive communication style, you might go on the attack if you don't get your way. These attacks may include sarcasm, "humorous" put-downs, intimidation, and humiliation. At these times, your sentences are likely to start with "You..." and include language that's blaming. An aggressive style also involves using absolute terms like "always" and "never" to communicate that you're right.

When you use this style, you can come across as superior and cold. Additionally, you'll be so intent on getting what you want and being right that you won't listen to what others are saying. In fact, you may not even care about what others are feeling or thinking. An aggressive style of communication may get you what you want in the short term, but it alienates others and casts you in a negative light.

Assertive

When you communicate with an assertive style, you make direct statements about your thoughts, feelings, and wishes. You stand up for yourself while also caring about and respecting the rights and feelings of others. You listen attentively and let others know that you've heard what they're saying. You can negotiate and compromise without dismissing yourself or your rights or violating the rights of others. You can hear criticism without becoming defensive or hostile. You can give and receive compliments. You can initiate and conclude a conversation. Your posture, facial expressions, and voice communicate openness and honesty. Assertive communication makes others feel like they can trust you because you're open and reasonable and you're "saying it like it is."

Exercise: Identifying Communication Styles

Now that you've read the descriptions of the three main communication styles, make a point of paying attention to the people around you or characters in movies and TV shows to see if you can identify their communication styles. You can usually see all three styles played out every day. We recommend taking some time to write in your journal about your observations and your reactions to these three styles.

Choosing Communication Styles

Ideally, assertiveness would be your primary communication style. That said, there are times and situations where people tend to use an aggressive or passive communication style—sometimes for good reason. The first step in choosing the most appropriate communication style is to look more closely at what distinguishes each from the others.

Reasons for Communicating in a Passive Style

The primary advantage to passive communication is that you don't have to take responsibility for your feelings or needs. Others can make decisions for you, take care of you, and protect you. That sounds pretty nice, doesn't it? Unfortunately, it's coupled with some significant disadvantages: loss of independence and repressed needs and feelings.

People also behave passively as a way to avoid conflict. You may see this as an advantage. But ironically, it actually creates conflict because others can become frustrated with your ineffective communication, and because you may get angry that your needs aren't being met. Alternatively, you might try to get your needs met in a covert way, which can leave others feeling manipulated.

As a teen, you're probably working toward independence. Because communicating passively makes you dependent upon others, this communication style is an obstacle on the road to independence.

✳ kelly ✳ I have twin brothers who are four years older than me. They've always asked directly for what they want: "Mom, I'm hungry. Can you please make me a sandwich?" In contrast, I would say to no one in particular "I'm kind of hungry" or "What do we have in the refrigerator?" When I was a kid, my mom would respond by asking me if I wanted her to make me something to eat. But this method of communicating started to frustrate her as I got older. My mom explained that most people won't care enough or take the time to explore my statements to find out what I really want. I realized that I needed to communicate what I was feeling and what I wanted. Sometimes I still fall back into my old, passive communication style, but I usually catch myself and switch into assertive mode when expressing my needs. Now I tell my mom that I'm hungry and would love to enjoy some of her delicious cooking. In this way, I'm communicating what I want in a respectful yet direct way.

Reasons for Communicating in an Aggressive Style

Aggressive communication can make you feel stronger and superior to others. When you're speaking aggressively, your primary goal is to win. And as mentioned earlier, you will win—in the short term. But you'll also come off as a bully, and eventually people will feel alienated by your style and avoid you if possible.

However, if you're ever in a situation where someone is making you feel uncomfortable or unsafe and won't leave you alone, an aggressive style of communication is probably appropriate— and even necessary. Here's an example: Say you're hanging out with a group of friends at a party, and you're introduced to someone new. The two of you have a short, casual conversation, then you go back to socializing with your friends. The person follows you and asks if you want to check out the backyard or go somewhere more private to talk. You politely decline the invitation, saying you'd rather stay with your friends and socialize. The person grabs your arm and pleads, "Come on. Why don't we just go outside for a few minutes?" This is the time to use an aggressive style, saying something like "No. Stop asking me to do something I've already said I'm not interested in doing. If you can't respect what I'm saying, leave me alone."

Setting Assertiveness Goals

Now you've read a few examples of situations in which using a passive or aggressive style of communication could be useful. Even so, you've probably come to see that an overall passive or aggressive style of communication would be ineffective over time and counterproductive for meeting your needs and developing successful relationships. Although we believe that assertiveness skills are essential to effective communication and successful relationships, it's important that you ask yourself whether it's worth it to you to change your communication style (assuming it isn't primarily assertive right now). To help you decide, ask yourself the following questions:

* What do I get out of being passive?

* What would I have to give up if I behaved assertively rather than passively?

* What do I get out of being aggressive?

* What would I have to give up if I behaved assertively rather than aggressively?

* What would I gain from being assertive?

Exercise: Setting Your Own Assertiveness Goals

In your journal, list at least five goals related to social situations in which you'd like to be more assertive. Write down the specifics of how you'd like to behave. List the people you want to be assertive with and explain why.

---

* kelly * Here are the assertiveness goals I came up with when I did the previous exercise:

1. I'd like to say no to friends when they ask me to hang out and I'd rather be at home.

2. I want to speak up in class discussions if I don't agree with the professor's opinion.

3. I'd like to tell my parents how I feel when they criticize me.

---

4. I want to feel comfortable telling a waiter that I didn't get what I ordered.

5. I'd like to be able to tell my brother that he needs to help with the dishes even when there's a football game on TV.

Expressing Yourself Assertively

For most people, direct communication is difficult. Maybe when you were a child, people told you not to talk about yourself too much. Or perhaps you're afraid that you'll be judged or rejected by others if you communicate directly about your thoughts or feelings. Whatever the reason, many people tend to communicate indirectly.

But when you communicate indirectly about your thoughts, feelings, and desires, you have to rely on others to pick up on your hints. If you're lucky and others are very attentive listeners, they may understand your thoughts, feelings, and desires or interpret them accurately. But why rely on luck? With assertive communication you don't have to.

In this section, we'll clearly outline how to communicate assertively. One key is that there are three parts to an assertive statement:

1. Your perspective on the situation ("I think...")

2. Your feelings about the situation ("I feel...")

3. Your wishes regarding the situation ("I want...")

Here are some examples of how to incorporate all three parts into an assertive statement:

* "We spend a lot of time talking about your relationship. I'm tired of only hearing about your problems and not having the opportunity to talk about me. I feel like I'm not interesting enough. And I wish we could talk about more than just guys we're interested in. I'd like us to talk about other things we have in common."

* "I think we have a lot in common and understand each other. It's fun getting to know you. I'd like to go out again next weekend."

* "Our family's been fighting a lot lately. I haven't been happy coming home because the environment is so hostile. I wish we could all be more mindful of each other's feelings. I hope we can sit down and talk about this."

You may have noticed that those statements don't use blaming or attacking language. This is crucial. When you describe the situation, focus on being objective. State the facts—what happened or what was done—without adding judgments. Don't make accusations that will put the other person on the defensive. Remember, the goal is to create an open and constructive dialogue. Also, be specific when you state what you want. This will help ensure you aren't ignored or misunderstood.

Exercise: Formulating Assertive Statements

For each of the assertiveness goals you listed in the previous exercise, write an assertive statement using the three-part formula:

I think…

I feel…

I want…

 kelly When I did the previous exercise, here are the statements I came up with for the five assertiveness goals I listed earlier:

1. I think you guys may feel offended if I say no when you ask me to hang out.

   I feel badly about turning down your offers to spend time together.

   Still, I want to find a balance between social time and "me" time.

2. I think that there's another way to approach this topic.

   I feel hesitant to express a different opinion because I value your opinion so much.

   I want feedback on my idea.

3. I think you may criticize me without thinking about how it affects me emotionally.

   I feel hurt sometimes.

   I want to receive more constructive criticism.

4. This meal isn't what I ordered.

   I feel badly that you'll have to do more work.

   However, I want to have the meal I ordered.

5. I think we don't collectively make an effort to get the chores done.

   I feel overwhelmed and a little resentful when I have to do our chores alone.

   I want to establish a rule that we do the dishes before we move on to our own activities.

When you find yourself struggling to express your feelings and desires, take a few minutes to write an assertiveness goal and a three-part assertive statement that you could use in the situation. This will allow you to be clear and direct in your communication.

Revisiting Active Listening

An important component of assertiveness is active listening, which we covered in detail in chapter 1. As a reminder, active listening means focusing your attention on others without interrupting. This will help you accurately hear their opinions, feelings, and wishes. To briefly review the specifics, there are three steps to active listening:

1. **Paraphrasing:** Use your own words to restate what the other person has said.

2. **Clarifying:** In this extension of paraphrasing, you ask questions until you understand what the other person is communicating to you: "I'm not really sure what you mean. Can you tell me more?"

3. **Feedback:** This is your opportunity to share your thoughts and feelings about what the other person has said. The key is to do so in a nonjudgmental way. Let others know that you've heard and understood their feelings and wishes. For example, you might say, "You're upset about this one issue, but I think there's a bigger problem that's creating conflict in our relationship."

Using Assertive Communication and Active Listening Together

Now that you've had the brief refresher on active listening, let's take a look at how to combine it with assertive communication. This is useful for those inevitable times when you're in conflict with someone and both of you have strong feelings. In this situation, the two of you would ideally take turns using assertive communication and active listening. This can clear up or minimize any misunderstandings and open the door to finding solutions. Here's an example from two college roommates.

Sean: Our room is a mess! I don't like coming back to this after a stressful day of exam review. [Assertive expression]

Anthony: I don't understand. Why are you so upset? [Asking for clarification]

Sean: I have to focus on my schoolwork, and I can't do that when our room is disorganized. Plus, it's hard to study when you have friends hanging out in here. I just want some quiet, please. [Clarification]

Anthony: I get that you're mad because it's loud and messy in here, and that you want my friends to leave when you're studying. [Paraphrasing]

Sean: Yeah, that's right. [Acknowledging being heard correctly]

Anthony: Well, I have my own priorities and things I need to take care of. My job at the student co-op is taking up a lot of my time. I didn't have time to take out the trash or vacuum today. I feel really overwhelmed trying to balance my academics, my job, and my social life. But I need time with my friends to de-stress from feeling busy all the time. [Assertive expression]

Sean: I hadn't realized how stressed you are. I understand where you're coming from. What can we do to help each other out? [Feedback]

Building from that conversation, in which they both used assertive communication and active listening, Sean and Anthony forged a compromise. They delegated chores and committed to doing them so that neither of them would feel their room was too disorganized. They also agreed to let each other know when it wasn't a good time to have friends over.

Exercise: Combining Assertive Expression and Active Listening

Ask a supportive friend or family member to work with you on combining assertive expression and active listening. Practicing this skill intentionally will help you use it spontaneously in real-life situations. When you practice, start with a small issue, such as deciding on an activity to do together. With time, you can move on to more emotionally charged issues.

Responding to Criticism

We are all unique individuals, with our own experiences, values, likes, and dislikes, so it makes sense that we won't always agree with each other. Sometimes disagreements result in criticism. Everyone has a difficult time hearing criticism, which we often associate with rejection and feelings of defectiveness. Of course, no one wants to be punished or rejected, so we create strategies to minimize criticism or the pain associated with it. These strategies include getting angry, lashing out, being silent, criticizing the other person, or agreeing with the person's criticism of you even if you believe it to be untrue. As you can see, those strategies are a mix of passive and aggressive approaches, and they can harm your relationships with others.

In contrast, an assertive response to criticism is based on the assumption that you're the final judge regarding your feelings, thoughts, wishes, and behavior. And, by extension, you're also responsible for the consequences of your feelings, thoughts, wishes, and behavior. Ultimately, you're the only person who can decide what's best for you. As you were growing up, your parents probably made most of the decisions about what was good for you because you were a child. But now, as you enter adulthood and develop important skills for building and sustaining relationships, you're the one to decide what's best for you.

Nonetheless, there will be times when others think they know what's appropriate for you or how you should be, leading to criticism. There are three good strategies for assertively responding to criticism:

* Acknowledging

* Clouding

* Probing

Acknowledgment

We can all benefit from constructive criticism, meaning helpful feedback that's intended to improve the situation and that's offered in a nonjudgmental way. It can help us improve ourselves. When you make a mistake (and we all do), receiving feedback can help you avoid repeating the same mistake. Sometimes people offer criticism that's accurate but not constructive. Either way, if you receive criticism you agree with, constructive or not, let the critic know he or she is right. For example, if you're rightfully criticized for not being punctual, you could say, "Yes, I'm late again, and I know it's inconsiderate to keep you waiting."

It can be easy to fall into the trap of apologizing or making excuses. Sometimes you may choose to offer an excuse or explanation for your actions, but this isn't necessary when dealing with friends and family members. In those situations, the important thing is to acknowledge to the other person that you made a mistake. When responding to an authority figure, on the other hand, you may want to add an explanation to your acknowledgment of the criticism. For example, in the previous scenario, about your punctuality, you might add, "The bus broke down and we had to wait for another one to arrive." In the end, whether or not you give an explanation, always acknowledge mistakes you genuinely made.

Clouding

Clouding is a helpful technique for dealing with unconstructive or manipulative criticism that you don't agree with. These types of criticisms may have a grain of truth in them, but they're intended to put you down. The key to clouding is to find something in the criticism that you agree with while inwardly sticking to your point of view. This is likely to calm the other person so you can talk about something else or end the conversation.

You may be wondering if clouding is manipulative. It is, but it's generally a better alternative than resorting to passive or aggressive communication. To use clouding, you need to listen carefully to the critic so you can find something that you agree with. Once you've done that, you can choose to agree in three different ways: in part, in probability, and in principle.

Agreeing in part: Find a part of the criticism to agree with and ignore the rest. Modify exaggerated words your critic uses, such as "always" and "never," rephrasing with a statement you can almost agree with but that doesn't distort the essence of the person's original meaning. Here's an example:

Critic: You're always studying. You think everything would fall apart if you took a day off.

You: Yeah, I do study a lot.

Critic: You never have time for friends anymore. You've become obsessed with your schoolwork.

You: You're right. I don't have a lot of time for my friends right now.

Agreeing in probability: If there's a chance, even a slim one, that your critic is right, you can choose to agree in probability. Continuing with the previous example, your reply might be "You could be right," "It may be that I study too much," or "It could be that I don't have time for my friends."

Agreeing in principle: You can agree with the other person's logic without agreeing with the premise. In other words, you can agree with "If X, then Y" and still not agree that X is true. Here's an example:

Critic: If you don't ever spend time with your friends, they'll drop you.

You: You're right. If I don't ever spend time with my friends, they will drop me.

Probing

There will be times when you won't initially know whether someone's criticism is constructive or manipulative, when you don't understand it, or when you feel like you're not getting the whole story. If you're in doubt or confused, try probing the other person to learn more.

First, identify the part of the statement that you think the person feels most strongly about. Then ask, "What is it that bothers you about [fill in the relevant criticism]?" If necessary, probe further by asking for a specific example. Listen carefully and continue to probe until you understand your critic's intention. Be careful to avoid questions and statements that sound defensive, such as "So what's the matter this time?" or "What's wrong with what I did?" Remember, you want to get the person to express his or her authentic feelings and wishes. Here's an example of effective probing:

Critic: You don't seem to put in a good effort when we work together. You do the bare minimum and then leave all the difficult, time-consuming stuff to me.

You: What is it that bothers you about what I contribute?

Critic: You always offer to do the easiest parts of the project, like compiling the presentation slides or printing out handouts. You get all the praise.

You: What bothers you about my work getting recognized in our presentation?

Critic: I'm frustrated because my efforts aren't acknowledged to the extent that yours are. I feel like I do more of the work, and I think you should offer to take on more of the effort.

You: Okay, I see where you're coming from. Thanks for explaining your perspective.

Exercise: Practicing Acknowledging, Clouding, and Probing

In this exercise, we provide several examples of criticisms. In your journal, write three separate assertive responses for each: one that uses acknowledging, one that uses clouding, and one that uses probing. We know this can be a little tricky, especially at first, so we've provided possible responses for each, in case you find that helpful.

1. "You're being really careless. We're not allowed to leave school grounds during the day. I don't care if everyone else does it. I feel like you're the most irresponsible person I know."

    Possible responses:

    Acknowledgment: "You're right. I am being pretty irresponsible."

    Clouding: "It's true that I like going off campus during lunch break."

    Probing: "Is there anything else that bothers you about my behavior, besides the chance of getting in trouble with the principal for leaving the school grounds? How else am I irresponsible?"

2. "You never seem to be invested in any relationship. Whenever there's any sort of conflict, you don't even try to work through it."

    Possible responses:

    Acknowledgment: "You're right. I guess I don't get emotionally invested with other people."

    Clouding: "It's true that I don't like dealing with complicated situations."

    Probing: "What annoys you about my behavior in relationships?"

3. "You spend all your time on basketball, either practicing, conditioning, or training on your own. It seems like nothing else in your life is that interesting to you."

Possible responses:

Acknowledgment: "Yeah, you're right. Basketball can get in the way of doing other things, like hanging out with friends or spending time with my family."

Clouding: "It's true, I do care a lot about basketball."

Probing: "What bothers you about my commitment to basketball?"

Special Assertive Strategies

When you need to set limits or assert your own needs in a situation, there are four special assertiveness strategies you can use:

* The broken record technique

* Shifting from content to process

* Delaying briefly

* Taking a time-out

The Broken Record Technique

When you feel like someone doesn't understand your message, or if you want to say no or set limits, you'll find the broken record to be extremely useful. You can also use this technique when others are so stuck on their own wishes or agenda that they can't see yours.

The broken record technique is useful for times when your explanation would provide the other person with an opportunity to make a bigger deal of a pointless argument. For example, maybe your sister wants to watch a horror movie together and you're terrified by horror movies, or maybe your boyfriend wants to go out for Mexican food and you'd prefer to go to a Thai restaurant.

The broken record technique is a five-step process:

1. Be clear in your own mind about what you want or don't want. Be aware of your feelings, thoughts, and rights relevant to the situation.

2. Formulate a one-sentence, easily understood statement about what you want. Avoid excuses and explanations. Be sure not to include "I can't," which begs for the response "Yes you can." It's always better to be simple, direct, and honest: "I don't want to." Finally, do a quick assessment to make sure that your statement doesn't include any loopholes that could further the other person's argument.

3. Use nonverbal communication to support your statement. Make eye contact, stand or sit upright, and keep your hands at your sides.

4. Calmly and firmly repeat your statement as many times as necessary until the person hears your message and understands that you aren't going to change your mind. Be consistent and persistent with your message. Eventually the other person will run

out of excuses and challenges. Don't change your statement unless the other person finds a serious loophole in it.

5. You may want to briefly acknowledge the wishes of the other person before you return to your broken record statement: "I understand that you want to watch a horror movie, but I'm not going to spend two hours of my life being unnecessarily terrified." Other than that, don't allow yourself to be sidetracked by the other person's statements.

One final pointer: If you're aware of particular people or situations that challenge your ability to say no or set limits, it's helpful to plan your broken record statements in advance.

Here's a dialogue that exemplifies the broken record technique:

Keisha: Let's go to the study session for history class this afternoon.

Joel: I feel pretty prepared for the test. I'd honestly just rather review the chapter tonight and study on my own.

Keisha: Our teacher said it would be really helpful for us to go to his review session. He may even give us a few hints about potential test questions.

Joel: I understand that, but I don't want to go.

Keisha: Well, I really don't want to go alone. I hope you don't miss out on anything because you're not coming with me.

Joel: I understand that you want me to go with you, but I don't want to go.

Keisha: It seems kind of stupid that you won't go to something like this with me. It's going to help you on the test.

Joel: I get your point, but I don't want to go.

Keisha: Fine, I get it. You don't want to go. I'll find someone else to go with me.

Saying the same statement repeatedly may feel awkward, but it works. Also, don't be surprised if someone tells you that you sound like a broken record!

Shifting from Content to Process

This will probably sound familiar: You start having a conversation with someone about a specific topic, but before long you find that that two of you have gotten off topic or that one of you is doing all the talking and the other person is silent. The conversation is no longer moving in the intended direction or toward achieving the objective.

In these situations, you need to shift from the agreed upon topic (content) to what's going on between the two of you (process). This skill involves a bit of self-disclosure about how you're feeling or what you're thinking about what's happening in the interaction. It's especially useful in situations where you feel the other person is expressing negative emotions ("Your face is turning red. Are you angry with me?") or if you feel the person isn't engaged in the conversation ("I feel like you're not really listening to me"). You can also use a content-to-process shift to express positive feelings that you're having about the conversation ("It feels great that we're being so open with each other"). The key is to make sure your comments are observational so others don't experience them as blaming or attacking.

Delaying Briefly

With texting, e-mail, and social media being such common ways of communicating, it's easy to get caught in the trap of feeling pressured to respond immediately—and expecting others to do the same. Feeling compelled to respond quickly is very common. A huge downside is that this can frequently result in agreeing to things we wished we hadn't or saying things we regret, usually because we haven't checked in with our feelings and needs.

Delaying briefly is a helpful technique that allows you to do four things: make sure you understand what the other person is communicating to you; think about what's been said; identify how you feel and think about the situation; and then respond in a way that leaves you feeling pleased with the outcome. In short, it gives you time to think about how you want to respond and prepare.

Of course, with electronic communication or social media, you can easily delay. But in face-to-face interactions, you may need to create a pause. Here are a few examples of how you can give yourself more time to respond in a conversation:

* "I'm not sure I understand what you're asking. Would you mind saying it a different way?"

* "That's a good point. Let me think about it for a minute."

* "Give me a moment to think. I want to find the right way to say how I feel."

* "Would you mind going over that with me again? I'm confused."

* "Let me explain what I took from what you said. Then you can let me know if we're on the same page."

Taking a Time-Out

You probably remember time-outs from your childhood. You may associate them with punishment. But really, a time-out is about taking a needed break during a situation that isn't heading in a positive or constructive direction. One situation in which a time-out can be helpful is when you need a break from the pressure of having to make a serious decision. Another is when communication has become too passive or too aggressive. Just don't use time-out in an attempt to avoid a conversation that's necessary but difficult.

Here are some situations in which you might want to use a time-out, along with examples of how you might express your request for a break:

* You're on the verge of tears and you can hear it in your voice. You're either anxious, embarrassed, angry, or hurt, and continuing the discussion would make your feelings even stronger. To take a time-out, you might say, "I'm upset, and it would be better for us to finish this discussion tomorrow, when I'm in a better frame of mind."

* You feel forced to make a decision and it's something you're not sure about. In this situation, you might say, "I'd like to think about this more and get back to you soon" or "I'm going to sleep on it."

* You're talking to a friend, coworker, or classmate who's being stubborn and aggressive. Here, you could say, "I think this is important, and I'd like to talk about it more tomorrow."

Putting It All Together

Using the assertiveness skills we outlined in the chapter may feel awkward at first. Sometimes it can be difficult to even imagine asserting yourself and your needs.

Reflect on the last time you felt unsuccessful in a conversation. Was the outcome what made you feel unsuccessful, or was it how you felt during the conversation? Did you hold back from expressing yourself because you were afraid the other person would criticize your feelings or reject you? Did you give in to the other person's decision or opinion because it felt like the easy way out?

If so, imagine yourself in a future conversation about something similar—a time when you need to communicate your feelings. Practice coming up with assertive statements, using words you can realistically imagine yourself saying, whether in a conversation with a friend, teacher, boyfriend or girlfriend, or family member. As you imagine saying these words, examine your body language—does it reflect your intent? Are you being direct with your feelings? Begin by practicing these skills with someone you're comfortable talking to, such as a close friend or supportive family member. With time, these techniques will feel natural to you and you'll able to use assertiveness skills in everyday life with a wide range of people.

chapter 7

Making New Connections

There are so many opportunities to make new connections in everyday life. Yet it can feel intimidating to start a conversation with a person you've never met before, or even someone who's familiar but you've never interacted with beyond a quick hello or a nod of acknowledgment.

Don't let fear of making contact get in the way of potentially rewarding new friendships and relationships. How many times are you going to pass that same familiar face without saying anything? You already know that you may share a common interest based upon where you run into this person, whether it's at an exercise class, a club meeting, or a favorite hangout spot. Are you holding back because you're afraid of being rejected? If so, consider the opportunities for connecting that you're missing out on because of reluctance to take a chance.

This chapter offers guidance in breaking out of your comfort zone and making connections with new people who can enhance your life experience. The advice we'll share can help you overcome limitations that are preventing you from broadening the many circles of your social network.

Overcoming Fear of Rejection

We all fear potential rejection when forging new relationships. It isn't unusual to wonder whether others will meet you with enthusiasm if you put yourself out there, or to feel like you won't fit in or won't be welcomed. Most people fear they aren't good enough, leading to self-consciousness. So when you see the potential to connect with someone new, you may immediately worry that the other person won't view you in the same way. This can make you more anxious about interacting, even in a simple conversation.

Given this very human tendency, you may be letting negative thoughts get in the way as you anticipate making contact with someone new. If you're worried, try reframing the situation. View making contact with someone as an opportunity, and focus on your curiosity rather than your worry. Also consider positive attributes you have that may appeal to a person you're thinking of talking to. Let's say you've seen someone a few times over the past week at a rock climbing gym. Your shared interest in rock climbing and being active could form a foundation for relating to each other.

Exercise: The Pros and Cons of Making Contact

When facing any challenging situation, including making contact with someone new, a helpful technique is to weigh the pros and cons. So consider the reasons why you'd like to approach a particular person and write about this in your journal. Then list the advantages and disadvantages of doing so.

* **kelly** * Here's the list I came up with when I was deciding whether to approach a guy in one of my classes:

Advantages

- The potential for a new connection, whether romantic or just a friendship

- Developing greater self-confidence

- Learning something new about myself

- Learning new things about someone else

Disadvantages

- The possibility of social rejection

- Initiating a conversation that doesn't go anywhere

- Being disappointed by what the person is actually like

When I weighed those pros and cons, I decided there are more reasons to go for it than not to. The possibility of rejection makes me anxious, but the excitement about a potential new relationship outweighs those negative feelings.

Being Realistic

Of course, no matter how enthusiastic or excited you feel about connecting, others may not always feel the same way, and it's important to be realistic about this. It can be helpful to tune in to the other person's signals to see whether it's a good time to connect. When approaching others, consider whether they seem preoccupied or in a hurry. There can be a variety of reasons why someone may not be emotionally present to engage in a conversation at a particular point in time. If you try to initiate a conversation while others are focusing inward or on other things, you probably won't be successful in initiating genuine contact.

That said, don't take seemingly unfriendly reactions as a rejection. Always keep in mind that there are many factors that might prevent a person from engaging with you or being receptive to an invitation, such as previous plans, state of mind, or mood.

✳ **kelly** ✳ There was a seemingly friendly guy, Wyatt, in my seminar class, and I'd said hi to him a few times. After one class, my mind was still racing about the discussion about Hamlet we'd been having. Walking down the hallway, I caught up to Wyatt and started talking to him: "It's weird that our teacher doesn't agree with your character analysis. Your point is really interesting and definitely has merit," I said confidently. Wyatt glanced over at me and mumbled, "Yeah, it's annoying," then took out his phone and continued walking. I felt embarrassed to have been dismissed like that. At the time, I didn't consider that Wyatt may have been distracted or upset. I just felt shut down.

The next week, I was pleasantly surprised when Wyatt took a seat next to me in class. "Hey, I'm sorry about the other day," he began. He explained that he was really irritated about how dismissive the professor had acted toward him and that he had just wanted some time to clear his head before his next class.

So don't interpret other people's less than enthusiastic responses as a reflection of how they feel about you. You can't read people's minds or be sure what issues they may be facing. Assume that a negative or indifferent reaction doesn't have anything to do with you. Ultimately, if an initial attempt at making contact isn't successful, don't be discouraged.

Guidelines for Making Contact

In this section, we'll provide several tips on initiating a conversation with a new person. We'll get into some specifics shortly, but first, we'll offer some general advice on how you can increase your chances of achieving successful interactions.

First, put into the interaction what you would like to get out of it. You may have grown up with the idea of the Golden Rule (Do unto others as you would have them do unto you), whether it was introduced by your parents, in an elementary school classroom, or perhaps by a camp counselor or babysitter. Consider implementing the Golden Rule in your conversations with new acquaintances. What do you want to get out of the conversation? How do you hope the other person will receive what you're saying and behave toward you? Keep these feelings in mind and treat the other person accordingly.

Second, focus on the conversation and the person you're speaking with. Although there's a natural tendency to prepare your next response while the other person is speaking, try to hold yourself back from doing that. You initiated contact with this person because you wanted to explore the possibility of connecting. Don't shortchange this potential by fixating on yourself.

And third, be mindful. Stay in the moment, focus on the interaction, and keep an open mind. Don't start anticipating what might happen next or get distracted by thinking about the future of the relationship.

Beyond those general guidelines, being aware of some specifics in regard to body language and breaking the ice can go a long way toward maximizing your chances of making a connection. Although you can't control how the other person reacts, you can increase the likelihood that you'll get a positive reaction by following a few simple guidelines for presenting your best self.

Be Aware of Body Language

Body language is often the first clue people get about each other. When your facial expression is friendly, your posture is upright and open, and you're making good eye contact, you welcome others into conversation. Making sure your body language is positive will help both you and others feel more comfortable and confident. If your expression is blank (or worse, negative), if you're slouching, or if your gaze is on something else, others won't feel your interest in getting to know them. So focus on how you present yourself, keeping these key points in mind:

* **Move toward the other person.** Close the physical space between you and the other person. If the person is seated alone across the room, walk over and pull up a chair. This promotes conversation and makes you appear friendly and self-confident.

* **Lean forward.** Lean toward the person. This shows that you're invested and interested in what the person has to say.

* **Have open posture.** Turn your body toward the person to reflect the focus of your mind and attention, and maintain an open posture to indicate friendliness and a welcoming attitude.

* **Make eye contact.** Looking at the person you're talking to is crucial in establishing a productive conversation.

* **Smile.** A positive expression will help the other person know that you're open and interested in making contact.

Use Icebreakers

The only way to start making contact is to say something. If you have trouble initiating a conversation with someone, you may be getting tripped up over what you should say. If so, you may find it helpful to think about why you want to make contact with that person. You might have a shared experience, like seeing each other at a coffee shop, perusing the same shelves at the library, or walking your dogs at the same park. This shared interest would be a great place to begin a conversation.

If you still feel stumped, here are a few types of conversation starters you might try:

* **Ask for information:** "Would you mind showing me where the auditorium is? I'm worried I'll be late to the first lecture." "Do you know when the next Hunger Games movie comes out? I've always wanted to go to a midnight premiere!"

* **Give a compliment:** "Those are really cool-looking running shoes. Are they comfortable?" "Your presentation on Kelly Slater was awesome. It made me want to learn how to surf."

* **Use humor:** "I can't believe how stressful signing up for classes is. I never would have thought I'd be so excited to get a spot in Biblical Literature." "Can I please share your umbrella? I already took a shower this morning!"

* **Reference current events:** "What do you think of Taylor Swift's new haircut? I know celebrity gossip is silly, but I can't help talking about it." "I barely slept at all last night. I was so excited after seeing the Warriors win."

Mastering the Art of Conversation

After making initial contact with someone new, it's important to consider how to engage in an interesting and satisfying conversation. Successful interactions rely on bringing together several skills discussed earlier in the book:

* Asking questions

* Active listening

* Self-disclosure

Asking Questions

There are two main types of questions that people use in conversation: ritual questions and informational inquiries. *Ritual questions* are used to open conversation. They focus on learning basic information about the other person. Here are a few examples:

* What's your name?

* Do you live in the area?

* Where are you from?

* Which school do you go to?

These questions give way to *informational inquiries*, which are designed to elicit detailed facts about the other person's experience, beliefs, and feelings. Here are a few examples:

* Who's your favorite NBA player?

* What's your favorite band?

* Do you like spending time in the city, or do you consider yourself more of an outdoorsy person?

* Have you ever had Mr. Levinson as a teacher?

Of course, it's important to be sure you're asking appropriate questions. You don't want to get too personal too soon.

Active Listening

We've covered active listening a couple of times already, so by now you know the drill: paraphrase, clarify, and give feedback (nonjudgmentally). Still, this is a crucial skill for successful conversations, so we'll revisit it here.

When you're having a conversation with someone, it's important for that person to feel that you're truly tuned in to what he or she is saying. So listen intently and be sure to show the other person that you're listening. The truth is, an inability to listen is the most common cause of conversational disasters.

Often, self-consciousness leads people into two traps: rehearsing and being preoccupied with fears of embarrassment or rejection. We discussed these and other listening blocks in chapter 1. But it will be worthwhile to review these two listening blocks here because overcoming them is essential for mastering the art of conversation.

When you're rehearsing, you aren't really listening to the other person. Instead, you're thinking about what you're going to say next. This is distracting and can cause you to miss parts of the conversation—which quickly becomes obvious to others if they're paying close attention. Focus on the other person and listen as if you're trying to memorize what he or she is saying. If you need to pause before you respond, that's fine; people generally appreciate a thoughtful response that reflects the fact that you were listening.

As for being preoccupied with fears of embarrassment or rejection, this is, of course, especially likely when you approach a new person. So remember, your chances for a successful interaction will increase if you can be fully present and engaged in the conversation. Plus, presenting your best self will actually help alleviate some of your fears. Finally, the more engaged you are, the more engaged the other person will be. We all value someone who is a good listener, and that means being an active listener.

Self-Disclosure

Now let's look at what sort of information to communicate about yourself. As discussed in chapter 2, this is called self-disclosure. Self-disclosure is fundamental to the development of any relationship. Sharing interests, feelings, and thoughts is what bonds people and helps them relate to one another.

We took a look at levels of self-disclosure in chapter 2. Now we're going to approach levels of self-disclosure from a different angle, thinking about it in terms of the stage of your relationship with the person: Are you just making initial contact, or are you starting to go deeper? It's important to keep these varying levels of self-disclosure in mind as you develop new relationships, whether with a new friend, a love interest, or an authority figure.

The First Level: Self-Disclosure During Initial Contact

When you first meet someone, you shouldn't reveal intensely personal things about yourself—and you probably don't want to! This can be off-putting to the other person and may create an uncomfortable dynamic. So at this stage, you'd probably want to stick with your interests and basic information about yourself. That said, it's also important to share things with the other person that reveal something about your character and what makes you unique.

Exercise: Brainstorming First-Level Self-Disclosure

For the first level of self-disclosure, think about some interesting facts about yourself. Really brainstorm and write your ideas in your journal. For this list, focus on basic information that you'd want a new friend to know about you.

✳ **kelly** ✳ When I brainstormed about how to engage in conversations when first meeting a new person, here are some of the ideas I came up with:

"I enjoy listening to live music. My entire family went to a Red Hot Chili Peppers concert, even my parents, and we had a great time together."

> "I'm very close with my older brothers. They have different interests and I love learning new things from them, like avalanche safety from my brother Jake, and the Giants' chance of making the playoffs from my brother Eric."
>
> "I love exploring the outdoors. On weekends I like to go on walks with my dad. It's a great way to spend time together while getting some fresh air."

The Second Level: During the Early Stages of a New Relationship

You can move to a deeper level of self-disclosure after you've made contact—sometimes fairly quickly after, depending on how the conversation is going. The second level of self-disclosure includes sharing your thoughts and feelings. Early in a relationship, it's probably best to limit this to thoughts and feelings about the past and future, such as sharing about your childhood or about your future career or school plans. Sharing your current thoughts and feelings can be difficult early in a relationship when you're still finding out about each other and building trust. It's a good idea to make sure you feel comfortable being vulnerable with the other person before sharing present-day thoughts and feelings.

Here are a couple examples of sharing on the second level:

* "I hope that I end up attending a university that makes me feel happy and fulfilled. I want to be involved in a fun, vibrant community. But I don't know if that's necessarily the school that my parents or college counselor will think looks best for getting hired after graduation."

* "Seeing this garden reminds me of the tomato plants my grandmother helped me tend as a toddler. That will always be a great memory of ours."

Exercise: Brainstorming Second-Level Self-Disclosure

For the second level of self-disclosure, think about some thoughts and feelings you'd like to share with someone who's becoming a new friend. Really brainstorm and write your ideas in your journal. For this list, focus more on thoughts and feelings about the past or future, rather than the present.

The Third Level: After a Relationship Is Established

Wait to enter the third level of self-disclosure until you've developed a trusting relationship. At this stage, you can begin to discuss present-day thoughts and feelings, including your thoughts and feelings toward the other person. Here are a couple of examples:

* "I've been enjoying getting to know you. You're such an easy person to talk to, and I feel like I can trust you. I appreciate your advice on my problems with my parents; it's been very helpful."

* "It's been so hard for me to deal with my friend's struggle with depression. I feel bad for complaining about it when he's fighting this problem, but sometimes I feel so helpless, like there's nothing I can do to make him feel better. I don't like feeling that way."

Since this chapter is on making contact, we won't offer an exercise for brainstorming topics for third-level self-disclosure, especially because what you share will probably vary widely from person to person. But if you feel like it, we encourage you to write some of your thoughts on this topic in your journal.

Putting It All Together

Making connections with new people and expanding those connections requires that you take a chance. If you use open, welcoming body language and appropriate icebreakers, and also master the art of conversation by asking questions, listening actively, and engaging in appropriate self-disclosure, you're likely to get people's attention. This can open the door to a conversation that just may be the start of a great new relationship. And if both of you combine asking questions with sharing information about yourselves, you'll both feel like you're getting to know one another.

chapter 8

Sexual Communication

Our culture has become so sexualized, yet few people are really comfortable having a discussion about sex. As a teen, you may find this topic especially challenging. You may face various obstacles in talking about sex, including shame, fear of rejection, lack of information and resources, judgments from your parents, fear of being bullied or ridiculed by your peers, and perceived power imbalances in romantic relationships. This chapter aims to help you feel more comfortable talking about sex and emotional issues related to sex, whether or not you're sexually active.

We'll address how to approach this challenging topic not just with your partner, but also with friends and family members. To be clear, this chapter is for all teens: those who are sexually active, those who are considering becoming sexually active, and those who simply want to feel confident and safe talking about sex.

Before we get started, we'd like to emphasize one thing: It's important to take your time when making a decision about whether to get sexually involved with someone. And along the way, you need to feel comfortable discussing sex, including both emotional and physical issues, with your partner. Make a healthy, positive decision by considering your values and your ability to communicate fully with your partner.

Identifying What Sexuality Means to You

In order to communicate about sex effectively, you first need to have a clear idea about what sexuality means to you.

When you love someone or feel a strong attraction, you may feel that the inevitable next step is to have sex. After all, that's what we see in the movies. So sex may seem like the most obvious way to show the other person that you care. But is that really true, or is it just the dominant message in our society? The fact is, there are plenty of nonsexual ways to express your love for another person. We do that in nonromantic love relationships all the time. Yet sometimes it can be hard to make a distinction between your true beliefs about something and the beliefs you've adopted, especially if you've adopted beliefs that seem to be common among people your age.

It may also be that you simply don't have enough well-rounded information to determine what sexuality means to you. Michelle learned a lot about this during an interesting conversation with a group of fifty college students. She wanted to find out how and what they learned about sex when they were younger, and what they were still learning.

Most of them had similar stories about learning the basics of male and female bodies, including sexual anatomy, when they were in elementary school. In most cases, boys and girls were separated for these talks (no doubt in an effort to eliminate the inevitable laughter that accompanies words like "penis" and "vagina"). Most of them learned a bit more in middle school, with further explanations of sexual organs, along with information about sexually transmitted diseases and pregnancy prevention. These students had clearly been on the receiving end of multiple levels of communication about the anatomical and biological aspects of sex. However, they agreed that they hadn't been taught much about the emotional aspects of sex.

This is widespread in our culture, and it's unfortunate. Your sexual health is comprised of both your physical health and your emotional well-being. Being emotionally prepared for sexual activity or a sexual relationship is essential. And part of that is being able to communicate how you feel about engaging in sexual activity with someone and what sexuality means to you.

Exercise: Reviewing the Sources of Your Information About Sex

It might be easier for you to identify what sexuality means to you if you examine the sources of your knowledge about sex. In your journal, take some time to outline what you know about sex, including both facts and beliefs. Also indicate the sources of that information. What did you learn from your parents? From sex ed in school? How about from friends or siblings? Did you learn anything from other sources?

After you've had a chance to process all of this information, think about what feels right to you, whether or not it aligns with what you've been taught. Do you feel clear about what sexuality means to you? Do you have questions about anything regarding sex? What resources do you have for answering those questions? If possible, go ahead and write some sort of description of what sexuality means to you. You can always revisit this topic later. It's likely that your ideas about this will continue to change throughout your life.

> *** kelly *** Due to the exposure our generation has to the media, I feel inundated with differing perspectives on sexuality. On some TV shows it seems that sex is a common activity for teens, both in and out of relationships. On other shows, the decision to have sex is portrayed as more complicated, which feels more genuine to me. My peers' opinions about sex vary as widely as the many messages I notice on TV and in the movies. I think the influence of the media on our attitudes toward sex is very powerful. We need to be discerning and review the messages we receive about sex, both in the media and in our lives.

Assessing Your Readiness

There are a few key prerequisites for healthy sex. One is free and enthusiastic consent. It's also important that the sense of power be equal between both partners. Mutual respect and trust are key elements of a sexual relationship, and part of that trust is being sensitive to each other's vulnerabilities. Of course, it's also essential that you and your partner agree about safety and the use of protection to prevent pregnancy and sexually transmitted diseases.

Exercise: Deciding Whether You and Your Partner Are Ready

Reflect on the previous section and write some of your key thoughts about it in your journal. Then, to fully explore whether you and your partner are ready to start a sexual relationship, consider all of the following questions and write your responses in your journal. These questions will help you examine your emotions and expectations around sex, and those of your partner:

- Have you talked about any religious or family beliefs that would conflict with a decision to engage in sexual activity?

- Do you both feel comfortable taking ownership of your emotions and actions, including feelings of sadness, regret, or dissatisfaction?

- Do you and your partner feel emotionally and physically safe with each other?

- Do you believe that your motives are appropriate and healthy, and that your partner's motives are in line with yours?

- Do you recognize that engaging in sexual activity could change the relationship, and are you prepared for those changes? Do you believe that your expectations are realistic?

- Do you have an adult you feel comfortable approaching for advice regarding sex? Does your partner have friends, family members, or other trusted people who can provide advice and support?

Your Values Regarding Sex

One of the most effective ways to get in touch with what sex means to you is to connect it to your values. If you can identify your values, you'll have a clearer understanding of your beliefs about sex and its role in your relationships.

At this point, you may be wondering, "What is a value, and how do I go about identifying it?" Values are principles that guide our decisions and actions. They tell us what to do, but more importantly, they tell us why to do it. They reflect our core beliefs and what truly matters to us. Values are also something we aspire to. There will be times when we will fall short of living our values. But when that happens, we can get back on course and continue to strive to make choices that keep us aligned with our values.

Another aspect of values is that they can be either personal or social. In this chapter we're talking about your body and your sexuality, so your values about this will be very personal to you. It isn't appropriate for anyone else to tell you how you should feel about sex.

> ✱ **kelly** ✱ I think it's important to examine your values in general before you approach any major decision. I ask myself, "How do my actions reflect my values?" If they don't seem to match up, does that mean that I'm making a mistake, or does it just mean my values are evolving as I mature and get older? I believe that people's values can

change as they gain life experience and their character develops. Because of this, I try to remember to check in and see how I'm feeling in the moment. Being aware of my emotions in a situation helps me make the best possible decision. Choosing to act in ways that are aligned with my values and beliefs helps me maintain my boundaries and make good decisions in difficult situations, including whether or not to have sex with someone.

Exercise: Exploring Your Values

There are endless lists of values (you can even just google "values"). The key is to identify which values are personally meaningful for you. To clarify your own values, read through the following list of words that encapsulate some common values. This list isn't comprehensive; it just covers enough areas to get you thinking about what really matters to you and what you value.

Acceptance	Compassion	Diligence
Affection	Confidence	Discipline
Appreciation	Connection	Drive
Approachability	Cooperation	Empathy
Attentiveness	Courtesy	Encouragement
Closeness	Depth	Energy
Commitment	Desire	Enjoyment
Community	Determination	Enthusiasm

Excitement	Inspiration	Respect
Expressiveness	Integrity	Responsibility
Fairness	Intellect	Self-respect
Faith	Intelligence	Sharing
Family	Introspection	Sincerity
Fitness	Joy	Stability
Focus	Kindness	Strength
Friendliness	Love	Success
Friendship	Loyalty	Support
Fun	Maturity	Sympathy
Generosity	Meaning	Teamwork
Growth	Mindfulness	Thoughtfulness
Guidance	Motivation	Trust
Happiness	Open-mindedness	Trustworthiness
Health	Openness	Truth
Honesty	Optimism	Understanding
Humility	Patience	Virtue
Humor	Perceptiveness	Vision
Imagination	Perseverance	Volunteering
Independence	Pragmatism	Warmheartedness
Individuality	Reasonableness	Wisdom
Insightfulness	Reliability	Zeal

In your journal, record the values that are important to you. You can either just jot down words from the preceding list or other words that capture your values, or you can write statements about the values you care about most deeply. Then consider how these values relate to your sexual life or the sexual life you envision for yourself, and write about this as well.

Effective Sexual Communication

There are many different contexts for communicating about sex, and your approach will obviously vary depending on who you're talking with and why. Obviously, discussing sex with your partner or a potential partner calls for a quite different approach than you'd take with your parents. Also, you may be seeking information, or you may want to share something about your sexuality with others. Any of these conversations can be challenging, so the sections that follow offer some pointers on how you might approach them.

We want to emphasize the importance of healthy, productive communication about sex in all of your relationships. Being able to discuss this topic, whether with a potential partner, with your friends, or even with your parents, is a fundamental step toward feeling more confident about your sexuality.

Communicating with Your Partner

Good communication will definitely improve any romantic relationship. It will also help you feel more assured about whatever decision you make regarding whether to engage with someone sexually. It's essential to communicate clearly about these issues if you're considering becoming sexually active with someone. Be sure to address these key points:

* Discuss safe sex and birth control.

* Be clear about your sexual and physical health and be sure your partner does the same.

* Discuss the pace you're comfortable with.

* Talk about what you want or need to be comfortable with intimacy.

* Discuss how you feel about your body.

* Communicate about what feels good and what doesn't.

* Discuss your beliefs and values about sex.

* Clarify how having sex may affect your relationship. For example, is monogamy a requirement?

Having healthy sexual communication means creating a space in which you and your partner can openly discuss what each of you want from your relationship and what does and doesn't work for each of you. Admittedly, this can be very difficult. Your partner may tell you something you don't want to hear, or you may need to communicate something that your partner might not want to hear. Healthy communication about sex means being able to say no and having your partner accept that with respect and without pressuring you to change your mind. It also means being able to say yes if that's the decision both of you arrive at after thoughtful, honest conversation. Although it can be challenging, communicating in this way will help you and your partner feel more comfortable together—or let you know that the relationship may not be a good fit.

Exercise: Planning for Effective Communication About Sex

Because talking about sex can be so challenging, it's a great idea to think about it in advance. This will help you formulate your thoughts and determine your preferences, and also help you communicate clearly when the time comes for a discussion. In your journal, record what you'd like to say to your partner about sex. If you don't have a partner, think about what you'd want to discuss and clarify with someone you were considering being intimate with.

Asking Questions About Sex

It's important to have the most accurate information possible about sex so that you can make healthy decisions. When seeking information, keep an open mind about who you might approach. Your partner, friends, or even family members can all be great resources for you. Though it will probably take some courage, ultimately you may feel more comfortable asking people you're close to about sex. We recommend turning to a trusted adult for advice and information.

In addition, you can find good information in books and even on the Internet. Just be sure to consult reputable sources, such as the websites of organizations like Planned Parenthood.

These websites provide information about sexuality in general, relationships, sexual health, sexually transmitted infections, birth control, emergency contraception, abortion, pregnancy, gender identity, and sexual orientation.

Talking to Your Parents About Being Sexually Active

Of course, it can be nerve-racking to even think about talking to your parents about sex. However, your parents can be a useful resource, and a good support system in making sexual decisions. After all, your parents have had to make similar decisions about sex in their own lives, and their perspectives and experiences can be informative. You might be surprised at how useful the conversation is, especially in regard to decision making.

Here are a few tips to help you feel more comfortable approaching the conversation:

* Pick a time when your parents aren't preoccupied and can give you their full attention. Understand that this may be a sensitive topic for them too, so make sure they aren't busy or worrying about something when you start the conversation.

* Set the tone. If you're feeling anxious about the conversation, feel free to share that with your parents. If you tell your parents that it feels difficult to approach a topic, they'll understand that you want to discuss something serious.

* Consider what you want to talk about and decide how specific you want to be. You can disclose however much information you want to your parents. At first, you might feel more comfortable speaking about sex more generally. For example, you could tell your parents that some of your friends have decided to have sex and ask them what they think about that decision. Then, once you feel comfortable and safe in the conversation, you could share that you and your partner are also considering becoming sexually active.

If you've decided to become sexually active and you're at a loss as to how to initiate a conversation with your parents about this, here are a couple of approaches you might try:

* "I'm thinking about having sex, and I want to talk to you about it. What do you think about that decision?"

* "I'm thinking about having sex. Can we talk about birth control?"

Talking to your parents about sex can feel intimidating, but they can probably give you valuable support and advice. However, if a conversation with your parents doesn't go well, or if you simply don't feel you can discuss this topic openly with your parents, find another adult you can trust—someone you would feel comfortable talking with about your sexuality and sexual activity. Later, this person may be able to help you communicate with your parents about your sexuality.

Your Sexual Orientation

Our culture is becoming much more open about sexual orientation. This has led to a proliferation of terms about sex and gender, and sometimes these terms get confusing. Basically, you have your biological sex, your gender, your gender identity, and your sexual orientation.

Biological sex refers to whether a person is female, male, or, in rare cases, intersex, with both male and female physiological characteristics. Gender can have several meanings, but it typically refers to social roles and cultural ideas about male and female appearance and behavior. It can also refer to a person's legal status. Gender identity refers to people's feelings regarding their gender. For people who are transgender, their biological sex and their gender aren't the same. In terms of sexual orientation, you may identify as straight, bisexual, gay, lesbian, questioning, or even asexual, meaning you don't feel sexual attraction to people of any gender.

These issues can be complex. They're also very personal, and a key part of your identity. No one else has the right to tell you what your identity should or shouldn't be. If you need support, or if you feel confused, seek out someone you trust and can talk to about this topic, or look for resources in your area. Don't struggle with these issues alone.

Putting It All Together

As you mature and consider becoming sexually active, it's important to have a solid understanding of the facts about sex, including about contraception and disease prevention. Be open to discussing these topics, as well as your sexual identity and decisions about sex, with your parents. If that isn't possible, find other trusted adults you can talk with about these topics. And remember, in addition to protecting yourself physically, you need to protect yourself emotionally, and to make sure your partner feels safe and protected. Ultimately, whether or not you're involved with someone or thinking about getting involved, it's a good idea to be clear about your values in regard to sex and to prepare yourself to talk about it.

chapter 9

Family Communication

A common desire that we all share is to be understood. With family members, many of us operate under the belief that they understand us better than anyone else, but this isn't always the case. And it may cause you to communicate less because you just assume they know your wants and needs.

Staying Current

As a teenager, you're in the middle of some of the most dramatic developmental years of your life. There's a high probability that some of the things that were true of you as a child have changed now that you're a teen. Or maybe your family members are assuming that some things have changed for you, but they actually haven't. Whatever the case may be, you need to maintain healthy communication with your parents and siblings so you can all stay current with each other.

Consider Mike's situation. When he started high school, he was so excited to be able to play football on the school team. In his freshman and sophomore years, he committed himself wholeheartedly to training year-round. Now he's seventeen and a junior, and he's noticed some changes in himself, including that football is no longer his priority. He taught himself how to play piano, and these days he prefers music, especially experimenting with different melodies and writing songs. While Mike still plays on the football team, he's more interested in devoting his free time to music. It's important for Mike to explain this change to his family so they can support him, and so they won't be making incorrect assumptions about what matters most to him.

Exercise: Understanding Your Changes

During your teenage years (and throughout life, really), it's a good idea to periodically assess yourself, identify ways in which you've changed, and communicate this information to your family members. In your journal, take some time to write about specific changes you've seen in yourself, including likes and dislikes, interests, values, and priorities. Also think about whether your parents and siblings are aware of these changes. Do you feel comfortable sharing them with your family? Whether or not you feel comfortable with this, spend some time writing about what you wish your family members knew about you. Expressing your observations and thoughts in your journal can help you feel more comfortable discussing these changes with your family.

Understanding Family Patterns and Communication Styles

Just because you live with people doesn't mean you know everything about them. It's likely that you don't give the same attention and focus to your family members as you might give to your friends. One reason is because your family members have been a more constant presence in your life. It's common to tend to operate on autopilot with the people we're around the most. Yet this can lead to incomplete or unhealthy communication.

Another thing that can affect family communication is people's communication styles. In chapter 6, we discussed three styles of communication: passive, aggressive, and assertive. Now we'll look at a few other styles to be aware of, especially in communications with family members. *Instrumental communication* is the expression of factual information, such as when you're to be picked up from school or the time and location of a game. This kind of information helps your family function in a more organized way. *Affective communication* is how people share their emotions, such as happiness, sadness, or anger.

You may have similar patterns to those of your parents, and if their styles are problematic (such as passive or aggressive), this can keep you or your entire family locked in a pattern of ineffective or difficult communication. If you've adopted your parents' communication styles, that's completely understandable. After all, you've been exposed to their habits since you were born. Like most people, you've probably accepted your parents' ways of relating without thought or analysis.

Alternatively, your communication style might be quite different from that of one or more of your family members, and this too can cause problems. Consider Daniel, whose family consists of himself, his older sister, Maria, and his father, Jose. Maria won't talk with anyone when she's upset—she doesn't engage in affective communication during difficult times. Like most parents, Daniel's dad makes the majority of the family's plans, and he's very open and direct with instrumental communication. But like Maria, Jose tends to be guarded about communication when he's experiencing negative emotions. Daniel, on the other hand, is very expressive and wants to talk when he's preoccupied with an issue. Unfortunately, his sister and father tend to shut down that kind of communication, which is frustrating for Daniel.

Exercise: Identifying Family Communication Styles and Patterns

Take some time to consider what does and doesn't work in your family's communications and write about this in your journal. Also identify the primary communication style each person tends to display and how all of the styles of communication we've outlined show up in your home. Do your family members use words to express affective communication, or do they tend to rely on body language or other signals? For example, do some family members clam up when they're angry? Spend some time writing in your journal about how each of your family members expresses instrumental and affective communication. Be sure to include yourself!

Do you notice any patterns? Do you have a communication style similar to anyone else in your family? Do your parents have the same communication style? If not, is it easier for you to communicate with one parent than the other? If so, why?

Family Rules About Communication

In almost every family there are some topics that are more acceptable to discuss than others. There may be spoken or unspoken rules about what family members can't ask for, talk about, or even just point out. These can become unconscious inhibitors that prevent you from sharing important parts of yourself and your experience. Here are examples of the kinds of communication that are off-limits in some families:

* Asking for help

* Seeking acknowledgment or recognition for work

* Asking for emotional support

* Showing that feelings have been hurt

* Showing any type of emotion

* Discussing sex

* Noticing or commenting on mistakes and problems

* Voicing disagreement or bringing conflict into the open

* Expressing anger, especially toward parents

* Expressing fear

* Showing affection

* Asking for attention

* Expressing ambivalence, reservations, or uncertainty

Of course, some topics can be more difficult to discuss than others. Yet you're also entering a time of life filled with uncertainties—a time of life when it would be ideal to learn to communicate your challenges, successes, and concerns to your parents and other family members. Perhaps you're entering junior high, high school, or college, and being able to talk with your family members about your experience would help you get the support you need in this new setting. However, it may be difficult for you to ask for certain kinds of help or guidance if you haven't done so in the past. And because of all the changes you're experiencing, you're also entering uncharted waters. You may feel uncomfortable bringing up topics that you've never discussed with your parents.

One thing to keep in mind when thinking about these topics or considering discussing them with your family is that your parents learned their patterns of communication from their parents. Styles of communication tend to be handed down from one generation to the next, and that could extend to you. The important point here is not to judge or blame anyone, but to bring your awareness to what's getting in the way of effective communication. By identifying areas in which you can make changes, you can improve your relationships.

Exercise: Identifying Your Family's Rules About Communication

Take some time to consider what rules your family may have about communication. Do any of them get in the way of you being heard and understood? And do any of them prevent you from being able to hear and understand your family members? Take some time to write about any rules that may be having a negative impact on family communications. Also consider whether you have any fears about expressing your emotions, desires, or needs with family members and write about this in your journal. If any of your fears are a result of past experiences that left you feeling emotionally unsafe or fearful of consequences from your parents or your siblings, be sure to write about this too.

✱ **kelly** ✱ I often feel anxious or reluctant to talk to my dad or brothers about things that are really upsetting me, whereas I always feel comfortable discussing a problem or venting to my mom. I think I assume my dad and brothers would be less interested in hearing about what's upsetting me. However, when I do reach out to them for advice, they're receptive and helpful. For some reason, I tend to forget that outcome and end up talking to my mom or a friend instead. This is why keeping a journal can be so helpful. Just by writing about this, I realized that this may be my own rule about what's okay to talk about, not a family rule.

Dealing with Expectations

Another reason family communications can be difficult, especially for teens, is because young people often believe their parents have certain expectations for them—and indeed, this is often the case. So you may fear disappointing your parents by expressing your true self.

Take Jason, whose father owns a hair salon, where his older brother and sister work. The business has always been a big part of the family's life. Jason grew up spending his weekends there, running around giving customers lollipops and watching his dad manage the salon. For years, Jason's dad has been telling him that he's a natural businessman and saying he can't wait for the day Jason starts working alongside him. Recently, however, Jason has been getting more interested in pursuing a future in acting. In fact, he's been talking to his drama teacher about applying for a performing arts scholarship. But even though this is his dream and very important to him, he hasn't mentioned it to his dad—or anyone else in his family—because his dad seems so excited about having Jason follow him in his footsteps.

Like Jason, you may be hiding a specific interest that you feel is in conflict with your family's expectations for you. Or you might find yourself in a situation like Casey, who's struggled with her sexual orientation. She's gay, but she's afraid to come out to her parents. She's an only child, and her parents have always told her that she was all they ever wanted, but that they'll be so excited to have a son-in-law when she gets married. She feels badly that they'll never get their wished-for son-in-law, and she feels so distraught about this that she's been unable to tell them that she's gay.

If, like Jason and Casey, you haven't been sharing your true self with your family, there's a good chance that you're really struggling. This relates back to chapter 2, where we discussed how important self-disclosure is for strengthening relationships.

If you've been hiding parts of yourself, you probably feel less connected to your family. You may even feel uncomfortable in your home, believing that if your family members knew the real you, they wouldn't love you as much or accept you as they do now. And the fact is, it can be difficult for parents to accept their children's growth and individuation.

As a teen, you're making dramatic changes—physically, emotionally, and socially. Parents often long for the time when their children were little and life seemed simpler and more predictable. When you were younger, it may have been easier for your parents to dream that you'd eventually fulfill their expectations. But in most cases, parents genuinely want what's best for their children. They want their children to live their own dreams. Consider Casey's experience. She did finally tell her parents that she's gay, and contrary to *her* expectations, they were happy and gratified that she shared this with them.

Exercise: Exploring Expectations

Have you hidden any parts of yourself from your parents or other family members because you fear they'll be disappointed? Do any of these fears stem from expectations you think your parents have for you? Take some time to write about this in your journal. As you do so, also consider whether any of your fears reflect your own expectations about how your parents will react. If this is the case, you might write about parts of yourself that you'd like to share with them, and about how you might approach this in a way that reflects your true self and your wishes, along with your concerns about disappointing your parents.

Common Communication Blocks in Families

In chapter 1, we discussed common communication blocks. Not surprisingly, many of these tend to cause problems in family communication. You can probably easily come up with examples of how advising, arguing, and being right show up and cause problems in your own family, especially in your interactions with your parents. These issues come up a lot as teens test their limits and become more independent. Another block that comes up often—and that may seem a bit surprising at first—is mind reading. Another is rehearsing.

Mind Reading

As mentioned at the beginning of this chapter, it can be all too easy to assume that your family members know everything about you or understand your thoughts and feelings, and vice versa. After all, your parents and perhaps your siblings have known you your entire life. It's easy for family members to fall into the habit of predicting or assuming each others' reactions and responses based upon past experiences and interactions. This assumption of familiarity can make active listening more challenging and lead to the misconceptions, misperceptions, and misunderstandings that result from not bringing full awareness to conversations.

✳ kelly ✳ My mom and I know each other very well—we talk every day and share a lot with each other. Sometimes one or both of us assume that we know what the other is thinking or feeling. A lot of times this works because we get each other. But it can cause problems in situations where either of us reacts or feels differently than the other predicts.

For example, the issue of mind reading in family communication came up between my mom and me when we were working on this book. We were talking about what to include in chapter 10, specifically the idea of bringing awareness to individual strengths and weaknesses when preparing for an interview. Here's how the conversation went:

Michelle:	Do you like the idea of including an example of identifying strengths and weaknesses?
Kelly:	I think it's a good idea.
Michelle:	It reminds me of the time Eric was in the hospital and we were talking about Jake's...
Kelly:	Yeah, I know, but I don't think we should use that as an example.
Michelle:	I wasn't suggesting using it as an example. I was just bringing up the story because it's funny.
Kelly:	Oh.

What just happened? In families, it isn't unusual to predict what other family members are going to say. We grow accustomed to hearing each other say certain things more than once. Then, when that seems to be happening once again, we may automatically take a shortcut to the end of the conversation. Unfortunately, we often jump to the wrong conclusion, which can derail a conversation.

Here's a classic example of mind reading. Esther, who's sixteen, wants to go to a concert with her friends on a Thursday night. In the past, her parents have expressed concern about her staying out late on school nights, and they generally haven't agreed to it. She decides to ask about this concert anyway, in the hopes that they might change their minds. When she brings it up, her dad's first response is to remind her why he's hesitant to let her stay out so late and get so little sleep on a school night. As Esther hears him saying this, she feels frustrated and starts talking over her dad, telling him that it's unfair that he won't make an exception this one time.

However, Esther's dad was just expressing his concerns before agreeing to let her go. Unfortunately, because Esther was mind reading, she started to argue before he was done speaking. As a result, he felt frustrated with her in return. Esther didn't give her dad the opportunity to tell her that he was willing to let her to go to the concert.

Rehearsing

Another common listening block in family communications is rehearsing. Let's revisit Esther's situation. When her dad started telling her he was concerned about her staying out late on a weeknight, she started coming up with arguments in her head. As she rehearsed how she'd respond, she stopped listening to her dad. And as you may have noticed, when she interrupted him to argue, she introduced a third listening block (arguing).

Putting It All Together

Everything you've learned in this chapter will help you strengthen your communications with your family and engage in more self-disclosure. In addition, we recommend that you revisit the concepts of listening with empathy, openness, and awareness, discussed at the end of chapter 1. When communicating with people you know very well, it's important to acknowledge feelings that may cause them to respond in a certain way, to listen without judgment, and to be aware of their beliefs or inquire about them.

chapter 10

Communication for Academic and Career Success

Most of this book has focused on communicating with friends, loved ones, or other social contacts. In this chapter, we'll look at how to communicate for academic and career success. While this is also a social realm, it typically calls for a different kind of communication. As mentioned in chapter 7, this kind of communication usually involves less self-disclosure. It also calls for presenting your best self. You'll definitely want to use active listening in these contexts, but you may want to be a bit more sparing in your use of some of the other skills in this book, such as assertive communication or challenging the distortions in others' perspectives. Of course, you should still be true to yourself. You may just need to tread a bit more lightly.

The Perils of Connectivity

These days we have so many ways to communicate with people—and to communicate quite quickly. While this creates more opportunities to connect, including in academic and professional realms, it can also lead to more miscommunication. So before we dive fully into communication for academic and career success, let's take a look at the potential advantages and pitfalls of some common ways of communicating.

Texting

Texting has made quick communication much more convenient. According to the Pew Research Center, 72 percent of teens text regularly and one in three teens send more than one hundred texts per day. Given these statistics, we think there's a good chance that texting is your favorite means of communication. There isn't much research yet on the long-term effects of texting on communication, but it is changing the way people communicate with each other. As you've probably experienced, it can create miscommunication because it leaves so much to interpretation. It also encourages incomplete sentences, misspellings, and less face-to-face contact. Finally, with so many teens using texting as a primary means of communication, it seems that many teens are becoming less comfortable with other forms of connection, such as phone calls, e-mail and other written communications, and, most of all, face-to-face interactions.

Written Communication

If you're in the habit of texting a lot, you're probably in the habit of abbreviating certain words or maybe even intentionally misspelling words. This is acceptable in texting, but it looks unprofessional or careless in other written communications. For example, Michelle once had a student turn in a paper in which he spelled the word "cues" as "Qs." This made him come across as lazy and perhaps less intelligent. In all of your written communications, give some thought to who you're contacting and how you want to present yourself. Make sure you express yourself in a way that conveys the message you want to send.

E-mail Communication

E-mail often falls somewhere between texting and formal written communication. It's versatile and an effective means of communication in many situations. But like texting, it can easily lead to miscommunication. As with other forms of written communication, it's important to keep the person you're contacting in mind and to adjust your style accordingly. Obviously, the style and tone you use with a close friend probably isn't appropriate for a teacher, boss, or elderly family member.

Whenever you write an e-mail, first ask yourself the following questions:

* Who are you communicating with? Is that person comfortable with e-mail? Does the person have regular access to e-mail?

183

* What is your relationship to the receiver of your e-mail?

* What do you want the person to think about you?

* What kind of impression are you trying to make?

Phone Calls

Effective telephone communication begins with thinking about your purpose before you make a call. What are you trying to communicate? If you don't reach the person you're calling, what message will you leave? Are you calling from a quiet place with limited distractions so you can focus on the conversation? Remember, every time you communicate, you leave others with an impression of you. Make sure it's a positive one.

✳ kelly ✳ I've found that it's very important to leave a voice mail if you don't reach someone. Adults especially seem to appreciate receiving a voice mail message. It can also make communication more efficient by avoiding the need to call that person back yet again. When you leave a message, you can go ahead and communicate what you want to say.

Face-to-Face Communication

Nothing replaces face-to-face communication. If texting or e-mail is your primary means of communicating, you're missing out on opportunities to make deeper connections. Both are great for quick, surface-level contact, but if you really want to connect with people, know them better, or have them know you better, it's essential to interact in person.

Self-Knowledge

You'll want to keep all of the pointers we've given in mind as you engage in academic and job- or career-related communications. It's also crucial to develop your self-knowledge. Because people you communicate with about academics or your career can play a major role in determining your fate, you need to present your best self. So to prepare for these interactions, develop a strategy based on solid self-knowledge. If you're being considered for any position—whether at a particular school, in a volunteer program, or for a job—the people you'll meet with will want to know that you have a keen awareness of yourself.

This may sound easy. Of course you know yourself. But do you know yourself in a way that you can communicate to another person, and in the context of the position you're seeking? Make a point of assessing your interests and skills. Then, as a first step, consider whether they're a good fit for the organization you're contacting and the position for which you're interviewing. Review the job description or other requirements and make a list of the skills and experiences you need to have. Then make a list of your experiences (in and out of school) and how these have strengthened your skills. Compare the two and consider whether they match up well. By considering this in advance, you'll be in a better position to provide examples of how your experiences relate to the position. You'll also be able to highlight your value to an interviewer.

Interviewing

For simplicity's sake, in the rest of this chapter we'll discuss interviewing for a job. However, all of the pointers we provide are also helpful when applying to schools or for volunteer positions.

Once you've determined that you meet the requirements for a given position, it's time to seek an interview. But first, ask yourself a few key questions to ensure that the opportunity is truly a good fit for you:

* Are you capable of doing the job successfully?

* Do you wholeheartedly want the job?

* Can you fit into the organization in terms of appearance and demeanor?

Dress for Success

Research the organization to find out if there's a dress code or how students or employees typically dress. When considering your appearance, keep these tips in mind:

* Arrive well-groomed, with your hair neatly trimmed and brushed, and styled away from your face if possible. For men, it's a good idea to be clean shaven.

* Don't use heavy fragrances, such as cologne or perfume.

* Don't wear a low-cut blouse or other suggestive clothing. Skirts and dresses should be no shorter than knee length.

* Don't wear open-toed shoes or heels higher than three inches.

* Keep accessories to a minimum.

As with your writing style, your grooming and attire communicate a great deal about you. What kind of impression do you want to make? If you're in doubt when dressing for an interview, err on the conservative side.

Types of Interviews

Depending upon the position, your first interview may take place on the phone, over Skype or something similar, or in person. In this section we'll provide some tips to help you make a good impression in all three kinds of interviews.

In-Person Interviews

It's common for an interview to start with the interviewer asking you to share a bit about yourself or to talk about why you're interested in the position or the organization. Make sure you're prepared to address this. Your answer should show how your skills, interests, and experience would be a good fit for the position and the organization.

The interviewer will want a fairly brief answer to this question, so consider using the following ninety-second guideline that many career centers suggest. Here's the formula:

* Focus the first fifteen seconds on any relevant and appropriate personal information you wish to share.

* Focus the next thirty seconds on your academic experience, such as specific areas of interest or relevant course work.

* Focus the next thirty seconds on your professional experiences, such as past employment, leadership positions, internships, or relevant extracurricular activities.

* Use the last fifteen seconds to emphasize your interest in the position, connecting this back to previously stated information.

Come up with a statement along these lines specific to each interview. Then practice your answer in advance so you can stay focused and concise. You might want to write a script to assist you when practicing. But when the time for the interview comes, set the script aside. You want your answer to sound heartfelt, not rehearsed.

Prior to the interview, also consider any questions you'd like to ask the interviewer. Make sure your questions reflect the fact that you've researched the company or organization. However, at this early stage, don't ask any questions about compensation or benefits. Those are only appropriate once you've been offered a position.

Be prepared in other ways, as well. In particular, be sure to bring any paperwork you may need with you. Have your résumé, the job description, and any other related documentation at hand.

Finally, end the interview well. At the end of the conversation, be sure to thank the interviewer for taking the time to talk with you. Reiterate your interest in the position, your belief that you would be a great fit, and that you would welcome the opportunity.

Telephone and Internet-Based Interviews

The preceding guidance on in-person interviews also applies to phone and Internet-based interviews. However, there are a few additional considerations when you aren't interviewing in person.

If you're applying for a position in a distant city or state, your initial interview may take place on the phone or over the Internet. Also, some organizations like to use a telephone interview to screen potential candidates prior to committing to an in-person interview. It's important to be just as prepared for these interviews as you would be for one conducted in person. This can be challenging, especially if you don't have much experience with Skype or conversing over the phone (maybe because you usually text!). Whatever your experience level, here are some tips that can help ensure a successful interview.

Act like it's an in-person interview. Of course, this is crucial for Internet-based interviews with video. But it's also important for phone interviews. Although the interviewer can't see you, you don't want to be in your pajamas in bed eating a cold piece of pizza. That would affect how you present yourself. So dress nicely and sit at a table or desk. If you feel professional, you'll be more likely to sound professional. If you have the opportunity, practice interviewing over the telephone with a friend to help normalize the process. All of this will increase the odds that you'll move to the next level of the interview process.

Test your phone reception or Internet connection. These days many people don't have landline telephones. If you're one of them and you'll be using your cell phone (or an Internet connection) for the interview, make sure you have good reception at the location where you'll do the interview. It would be both unfortunate and unprofessional if your phone were to drop the call in the middle of the conversation. If you're using your cell phone, make sure any incoming texts or calls are muted so notifications won't disrupt the call.

Eliminate background noise. Make sure your location is quiet and private. Do whatever you can at your end to make sure that both you and the interviewer have as few distractions as possible.

> ✳ **kelly** ✳ I recently interviewed over the phone for a part-time job at a fitness studio. I followed many of this chapter's guidelines. For example, I set myself up in a quiet room, seated at a desk with my résumé and the job description in front of me. I wrote down a few key points before the interview began, including some of my interests that relate to the position, such as leading a healthy, active lifestyle. This helped me feel prepared and confident during the interview.

After the Interview

Whether you interview by phone or in person, as soon as possible after the interview send a thank-you note to the interviewer. In your note, reiterate your interest in the position. Mention something specific about the interview, or consider clarifying something you weren't able to fully communicate during the interview. Keep your note brief. If a decision about the position is being made immediately, send your thank-you note by e-mail. If there's more time, sending a formal, hand-written thank-you note is a nice touch. Either way, express your appreciation for the time the person took to interview you. Hopefully it goes without saying that your spelling and grammar should be impeccable.

The Little Things That Matter

We have a final bit of advice about academic- and career-related communications: Pay attention to the small stuff. You might be thinking, "Why would this be a big deal? It's called 'small stuff' for a reason." That's true, in a sense, but little things *do* matter and they don't go unnoticed. Again, all of your actions and communications—even the minor ones—say something about you. To help you attend to the small stuff, keep these pointers in mind:

* Show up. It doesn't matter how elaborate or creative your excuses are for not attending class or going to work. If you make a habit of not showing up, you'll get a reputation for not being dependable. Ultimately, people may not trust you.

* Be on time. If you're chronically late, it sends a message that you don't care.

* Follow through. If you start something or commit to something, finish it.

* Respond quickly. Don't leave people hanging. Again, this makes it seem like you don't care.

* Say "please" and "thank you." This is simple to do and shows that you care about consideration and manners, which is likely to distinguish you from quite a few other teens.

When you do these "little" things, people will notice. Later, they'll think of you when they need someone who's respectful, dependable, conscientious, and detail oriented.

Putting It All Together

Beyond the pointers we've offered in this chapter, you can find many interviewing resources online and in schools and libraries. Keep in mind that every form of communication is a representation of who you are. To truly put your best foot forward, ask a friend, parent, or teacher to role-play interviews with you to help you prepare. If you're not confident about your writing skills, ask someone whose ability you respect to review your paperwork for clarity and any spelling or grammar errors. Remember, anyone who's evaluating you and considering you for any type of position will notice preparation and attention to detail on your part.

Conclusion

Your well-being depends upon your relationships. The key to healthy, loving, and fulfilling relationships is effective communication. You can communicate more effectively when you have a good understanding of yourself and are interested in others and open to understanding them. After all, we communicate in order to be understood and to understand others. For this to happen, you need to express yourself well and listen well. You need to be aware of your listening blocks and work to overcome them, and try to listen without judgment. You won't always agree with others' perspectives (or they with yours), but you can endeavor to understand the people in your life. The skills and tools for effective communication that you've learned in this book will help you create deeper, more meaningful, and more successful connections with others. We wish you all the best in your communications, your relationships, and your life!

Michelle Skeen, PsyD, is a therapist who lives and works in San Francisco, CA. She has provided brief and long-term therapy for individuals and couples by utilizing schema and mindfulness-based approaches to address interpersonal issues, weight management, anger, depression, anxiety, disabilities, and trauma. She is author of *Love Me, Don't Leave Me* and coauthor of *Acceptance and Commitment Therapy for Interpersonal Problems*. Skeen hosts a weekly radio show called *Relationships 2.0 with Dr. Michelle Skeen* on KCAA 1050 AM. To find out more, visit her website at www.michelleskeen.com.

LisaKeatingPhotography.com

Matthew McKay, PhD, is a professor at the Wright Institute in Berkeley, CA. He has authored and coauthored numerous books, including *The Relaxation and Stress Reduction Workbook*, *Self-Esteem*, *Thoughts and Feelings*, *When Anger Hurts*, and *ACT on Life Not on Anger*. He's also penned two novels: *Us* and *Wawona Hotel*. McKay received his PhD in clinical psychology from the California School of Professional Psychology, and specializes in the cognitive behavioral treatment of anxiety and depression. He lives and works in the San Francisco Bay Area.

Patrick Fanning is a professional writer in the mental health field, and founder of a men's support group in Northern California. He has authored and coauthored eight self-help books, including *Self-Esteem, Thoughts and Feelings, Couple Skills,* and *Mind and Emotions.*

Kelly Skeen is a student at Georgetown University in Washington, DC.

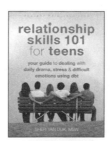